Shakespeare's Creative Legacies

RELATED TITLES

On Shakespeare's Sonnets: A Poet's Celebration **edited by Hannah Crawforth and Elizabeth Scott-Baumann**

Performing King Lear: Gielgud to Russell Beale, **Jonathan Croall**

Shakespeare in Our Time: A Shakespeare Association Collection **edited by Dympna Callaghan and Suzanne Gossett**

Shakespeare's Creative Legacies

Artists, Writers, Performers, Readers

**Edited by Paul Edmondson
and Peter Holbrook**

Bloomsbury Arden Shakespeare
An imprint of Bloomsbury Publishing Plc

BLOOMSBURY
LONDON · OXFORD · NEW YORK · NEW DELHI · SYDNEY

Bloomsbury Arden Shakespeare
An imprint of Bloomsbury Publishing Plc

Imprint previously known as Arden Shakespeare

50 Bedford Square	1385 Broadway
London	New York
WC1B 3DP	NY 10018
UK	USA

www.bloomsbury.com

BLOOMSBURY, THE ARDEN SHAKESPEARE and the Diana logo are trademarks of Bloomsbury Publishing Plc

First published 2016

© Paul Edmondson, Peter Holbrook and contributors 2016
John Ashbery's contribution © John Ashbery 2016. All rights reserved. Used by arrangement with Georges Borchardt, Inc.

The editors and contributors have asserted their right under the Copyright, Designs and Patents Act, 1988, to be identified as author of this work.

All rights reserved. No part of this publication may be reproduced or transmitted in any form or by any means, electronic or mechanical, including photocopying, recording, or any information storage or retrieval system, without prior permission in writing from the publishers.

No responsibility for loss caused to any individual or organization acting on or refraining from action as a result of the material in this publication can be accepted by Bloomsbury or the author.

British Library Cataloguing-in-Publication Data
A catalogue record for this book is available from the British Library.

ISBN: HB: 978-1-4742-3449-8
PB: 978-1-4742-3448-1
ePDF: 978-1-4742-3451-1
ePub: 978-1-4742-3450-4

Cover design by Dani Leigh
Cover image *Ariel* by John Link www.johnlink.co.uk

Typeset by Fakenham Prepress Solutions, Fakenham, Norfolk, NR21 8NN

This book is dedicated to the members of the International Shakespeare Association, a UK-based charity furthering the study of Shakespeare's life and work.

All proceeds from the sale of the book will be donated to the Association.
(reg. charity no. 1160312)

Contents

Acknowledgements ix
Foreword by Stanley Wells x
Notes on Contributors xiii

Torn from Shakespeare's Journal xvi
Roger Pringle

Introduction: Great Creating Shakespeare 1
Paul Edmondson and Peter Holbrook

Part One: Essays 9

1. Shakespeare and the Theatre 11
   Paul Prescott

2. Shakespeare and Poetry 27
   Sukanta Chaudhuri

3. Shakespeare and Music 47
   Tom Bishop

4. Shakespeare and Dance 61
   David Fuller

5. Shakespeare and Opera 79
   Penny Gay

6. Shakespeare and the Novel 93
   Graham Holderness

7. Shakespeare and Film and Television 107
   Russell Jackson

Part Two: Further Reflections 119

John Ashbery – Shaul Bassi – Simon Russell Beale – Sally Beamish – David Bintley – Michael Bogdanov – Kenneth Branagh – Debra Ann Byrd – John Caird – Antoni Cimolino – Wendy Cope – Gregory Doran – Margaret Drabble – Dominic Dromgoole – Ellen Geer – Michael Holroyd – Gordon Kerry – John Kinsella – Juan Carlos Liberti – Lachlan Mackinnon – David Malouf – Javier Marías – Yukio Ninagawa – Janet Suzman – Salley Vickers – Rowan Williams – Lisa Wolpe – Greg Wyatt

Shakespeare's Legacy of Storytelling 165
Indira Ghose

William Shakespeare: 1616–2016 178
Paul Edmondson

Acknowledgements

The editors gratefully acknowledge the support of the many people who assisted in the planning and preparation of this book, in particular: Margaret Jull Costa, Christine Edwards, Jo Hornsby, Akiko Kusunoki, Bronwyn Lea, Kazuko Matsuoka, Richard Newman, Meg Poole and Tamar Thomas. Mercedes de la Torre and Carlos A. Drocchi of the Fundación Shakespeare Argentina were very helpful in enabling us to include reference to the paintings of Juan Carlos Liberti. Xanthe Ashburner, Peter Holbrook's colleague at the University of Queensland, gave indispensable and astute advice at every stage of the project. We are immensely grateful to Margaret Bartley, our editor at Bloomsbury for the Arden Shakespeare, for her patience and encouragement, and for first suggesting the project to us. Finally, we should like to thank all of the contributors to this book, whose work has been donated gratis in order to support the aims of the International Shakespeare Association.

Foreword

This is a book of enthusiasms – about enthusiasm as a response to works of art – specifically to the plays and poems of William Shakespeare – and enthusiasm for Shakespeare as a stimulus to the creation of further works of art in many different genres. It applies to Shakespeare himself Falstaff's often-quoted claim that he is 'not only witty in' himself 'but the cause that wit is in other men' (*King Henry IV*, Part 2, 1.2.9-10).

In the first part of the book – which itself is framed by two Shakespeare-inspired poems – an appropriately international team of contributors offer wonderfully well-informed but concise and critically astute surveys of the impact that enthusiasm for Shakespeare has exerted, and goes on exerting, on creative artists 'in states unborn and accents yet unknown' to Shakespeare himself (*Julius Caesar*, 3.1.113). The editors' Introduction offers a thoughtful and illuminating discussion of what it is within Shakespeare's works themselves that can explain the impact they have had on artistic creativity, interestingly and provocatively quoting Wittgenstein's suggestion that this arises partly because of an unfinished quality within the plays. In a sense this is inevitably true of any works written to be performed, which are incomplete until other artists – actors, musicians, designers, directors and so on – have made their contribution. It also explains why any play is to some extent a different work of art whenever it is performed. Paul Prescott's chapter on Shakespeare and the theatre looks at the many different ways in which the plays have been 'creatively refashioned and reproduced ... in their natural habitat, the theatre', sometimes departing so radically from their original form as to constitute independent works of art in their own right.

And Shakespeare's works – poems as well as plays – have provided inspiration to artists in many genres other than the drama. Sukanta Chaudhuri's essay on Shakespeare and poetry ranges widely both geographically and generically in its critical survey of how Shakespeare has been 'so variously naturalized in the total universe of the world's poetry'. Non-verbal arts, too, have reflected Shakespeare's influence. Tom Bishop explores Shakespeare-inspired music over the centuries and David Fuller investigates the paradox of Shakespeare-without-words that underlies balletic versions of the plays – and even ballets inspired by the poems: here, he suggests, we may see the plays in ways that Shakespeare himself rarely saw them, 'as narrative structure, embodied movement, sequence[s] of tones and tableaux, and emblematic stage picture[s]'. Operatic versions of Shakespeare, discussed by Penny Gay, along with screen adaptations on both film and television, illuminated by Russell Jackson, bring us closer to the medium for which the plays were originally written, whereas Graham Holderness demonstrates the impact that novelists' enthusiasm for Shakespeare has exerted on their work in many different cultures.

In the book's second part, numerous practitioners of the arts – poets, composers, actors, directors, novelists, and visual artists – tell us, some of them in affectingly intimate terms, about the origins of their enthusiasm for Shakespeare, and explore the effect it has had on their lives and work. And, in the closing chapter, 'Shakespeare's Legacy of Storytelling', Indira Ghose returns to the theme of what it is that makes Shakespeare so 'amenable to reinterpretation', suggesting that this results from the absence from his plays of 'moral closure', so that 'they appeal to the autonomy of spectators, requiring them to draw their own conclusions'. The wide international spread of the contributors to this book is in itself an indication of the breadth of Shakespeare's global appeal, which has made itself manifest over the centuries in ways that have increased exponentially with the development in recent times of new media and fresh modes of transmission.

Among the many manifestations of enthusiasm for Shakespeare over the years has been the work of the International Shakespeare Association, which publication of this book supports. Since it was founded in 1974, the ISA has done much to further worldwide appreciation and understanding of Shakespeare, especially through its organization of a series of World Shakespeare Congresses, held at five-yearly intervals in many cities of the world since 1974, and of which, as a former Chairman, I have long experience. The Congresses, open to members of the general public as well as to professional academics, have regularly invited contributions from creative artists, demonstrating their enthusiasm for Shakespeare, and discussing the effect this has had on their work.

Stanley Wells
Honorary President, The Shakespeare Birthplace Trust
Vice-President, International Shakespeare Association

Notes on Contributors

Tom Bishop is Professor of English at the University of Auckland, where he teaches in English and Drama. He is the author of *Shakespeare and the Theatre of Wonder* (Cambridge University Press, 1996), the translator of Ovid's *Amores* (Carcanet, 2003) and a General Editor of *The Shakespearean International Yearbook*, an annual volume of scholarly essays published by Ashgate.

Sukanta Chaudhuri is Professor Emeritus at Jadavpur University. He is author of *Infirm Glory: Shakespeare and the Renaissance Image of Man* (Clarendon Press, 1981), *Renaissance Pastoral and Its English Developments* (Clarendon Press, 1989), *Translation and Understanding* (Oxford University Press, 1999), and *The Metaphysics of Text* (Cambridge University Press, 2010) and editor of the Third Arden *Midsummer Night's Dream* and *Pastoral Poetry of the English Renaissance* (Manchester University Press, 2016). He co-ordinated *Bichitra*, the Tagore Online Variorum.

Paul Edmondson is Head of Research and Knowledge and Director of the Stratford-upon-Avon Poetry Festival for The Shakespeare Birthplace Trust. His *Shakespeare: Ideas in Profile* was published by Profile Books in 2015. He is a Trustee for The British Shakespeare Association and Chair of the Hosking Houses Trust for women writers. @paul_edmondson

David Fuller is Emeritus Professor of English at the University of Durham, and former University Orator. He has written on subjects from medieval to contemporary, particularly Marlowe, Shakespeare and the Renaissance, Blake and the Romantic period, and Joyce and Modernism. He trained as a musicologist, and plays the piano and organ.

Penny Gay is Professor Emerita in English Literature and Drama at the University of Sydney. She has published extensively on Shakespeare, including a new Introduction to *Twelfth Night* for the New Cambridge Shakespeare (2016). Her research on performance history includes a particular interest in the power of music and song.

Indira Ghose is Professor of English at the University of Fribourg in Switzerland. Her book *Shakespeare and Laughter: A Cultural History* appeared with Manchester University Press in 2008. She is currently working on a book on Renaissance courtesy literature and the theatre.

Peter Holbrook is Professor of English Renaissance Literature at the University of Queensland, and Director of the UQ Node of the Australian Research Council Centre of Excellence for the History of Emotions (Europe 1100–1800). His most recent book is *English Renaissance Tragedy: Ideas of Freedom* (Arden Shakespeare, 2015), and he is currently Chair of the International Shakespeare Association.

Graham Holderness has published over forty books and hundreds of chapters and articles on literature, theory and theology. These include, most recently, *Nine Lives of William Shakespeare* (Arden Shakespeare, 2011), *Tales from Shakespeare: Creative Collisions* (Cambridge University Press, 2014), *Re-writing Jesus: Christ in Twentieth-Century Fiction and Film* (Bloomsbury, 2014), and the Shakespearean novels *The Prince of Denmark* (University of Hertfordshire Press, 2001) and *Black and Deep Desires: William Shakespeare, Vampire Hunter* (Top Hat Books, 2015).

Russell Jackson is Allardyce Nicoll Professor of Drama in the University of Birmingham. His most recent publications include *The Cambridge Companion to Shakespeare on Film* (second edition, 2007), *Shakespeare Films in the Making: Vision, Production and Reception* (Cambridge University Press, 2007), *Theatres on Film: How the Cinema Imagines the Stage* (Manchester University Press, 2013) and *Shakespeare and the English-speaking Cinema* (Oxford University Press, 2014).

Paul Prescott is Reader in English at the University of Warwick. He is the author of *Reviewing Shakespeare* (Cambridge University Press, 2013); a critical biography of Sam Wanamaker for the *Great Shakespeareans* series (Arden, 2013); and, as co-editor and contributor, *A Year of Shakespeare* and *Shakespeare on the Global Stage* (Arden, 2013 and 2014).

Torn from Shakespeare's Journal

Roger Pringle

This recently found manuscript appears to be the only portion to have survived of a journal kept by the dramatist. It is likely these final entries were extracted at an early period, before being consigned to a trunk in an attic of an old mansion, near Stratford.

An edition with full scholarly appendage is expected soon from a leading university press.

Monday, 17 April
Old friend Ben stayed the night and talked non-stop,
a merry meeting of sorts, I knocked back
five pots of ale, though he demolished nine,
but I've small interest now in London gossip;
full of his plans to publish all his work,
urged me likewise: told him I'll give it thought.

Tuesday, 18 April
Noticed a martin leave its mud-bound nest
under the barn's eaves, where we store the malt:
I wonder if it slept out winter there.
Consulted Hall about some purple spots
erupting in a private place last week,
I don't expect his unguent's any good.

Wednesday, 19 April
Quarrelled with Anne on details of my will,
who'd be bequeathed the best bed, etc.,
assured her she'd be well provided for.

We seemed to stitch things up, for later on
she cooked my favourite dish of venison,
known in our house as 'Charlecote poacher pie'.
I'll leave my sword to young-limbed, neighbour Combe
and ten pounds, I suppose, for Stratford's poor.

Thursday, 20 April
Carrier brings a letter from Dick Burbage;
good news of post-Lent takings at the Globe,
and Lear to be revived, though B now asks
for further changes, which pleases me not;
the script's been resting since before the time
I took my dearest daughter up the aisle.
Spring is intolerably late this year
but daffodils begin at last to peer
around our courtyard corner near the well.

Friday, 21 April
Went for a walk along the river bank,
the Avon sluggish, ditto all my thoughts;
will work with Fletcher still, no solo plays,
too tired, not well, what else is there to say.
The willows breaking into yellow leaf
brought back those springs when I with other lads
swam out like mad and put the swans to flight.
Somewhere today I dropped my signet ring:
feel its loss more than reason should allow.

Saturday, 22 April
Knot garden full of weeds, I pulled them out;
must ask George Bardolfe to repair the wall
where last year's dangling apricots did well.
Pains in the legs and those spots getting worse.
Another tax demand for road repairs,
is there no end to emptying of my purse?

Torn from Shakespeare's Journal

Sunday, 23 April
Sermon too long, and life too short. No spur
to bring the plays together in one book.
I rowed again with Judith over Quiney,
said she'd been mental marrying such a knave,
she slammed the door and cracked its wainscot-work;
who am I to tell her about false love?
It's been my birthday, friends and family supped
(venison, once more), tried to show some cheer,
Susanna, radiant, gave a witty toast;
left them to it, the candles now all out.

Introduction: Great Creating Shakespeare

Paul Edmondson and Peter Holbrook

The art itself is nature.
THE WINTER'S TALE, 4.4.97

Four hundred years on from the beginning of one of the strongest of all artistic legacies, we – artists, writers, performers and readers – continue to create and re-create Shakespeare. Why? Some explanations are obvious: the sheer unmatched eloquence of the writing; the cultural prestige of the works in many parts of the world; the sticking quality – the memorableness – of Shakespeare's stories, characters and incidents; the intellectual adventurousness and range of the plays; their refusal of oversimplification. All of these are reasons for Shakespeare's influence on numberless poets, novelists, dramatists, composers, painters, directors, filmmakers and performers.

But perhaps another explanation for Shakespeare's impact on artistic creativity, one less frequently encountered, is to be found in an insight of the philosopher Ludwig Wittgenstein. Wittgenstein confessed honestly to, and was puzzled by, his own unresponsiveness to Shakespeare, drawing attention to what he called the plays' sketchiness: 'His pieces give me an impression', Wittgenstein wrote, 'as of enormous *sketches* rather than of paintings; as though they had been *dashed off* by someone who can permit himself *anything*, so to speak'.

Shakespeare's works as 'enormous sketches'? Wittgenstein's observation may well strike us as itself a mere sketch, grossly impressionistic and crying out for clarification and not a little qualification. For a start, he does not make it clear to which plays he is referring: some are clearly more finished than others and Shakespeare would probably be the first to admit it. More broadly, we might reasonably object to characterizing works as powerful and unforgettable as *Macbeth* or *Twelfth Night* as 'sketches'. Surely they are fully worked-up canvases rather than preliminary attempts – massively *there*, utterly different one from another and as seemingly real as the world itself. We often speak of Shakespeare's characters as though they were flesh-and-blood people: in the later seventeenth century the poet Margaret Cavendish claimed that Shakespeare's 'persons' were so convincing that 'one would think he had been transformed into everyone of [them] he hath described'. The vivid actualities of such masterpieces as *King Lear* or *Hamlet* are generated by an artistry much more substantial than that of a casual, gestural 'sketch'.

But what Wittgenstein seems to have meant by 'sketchiness' was not artlessness, part- or ill-formedness – as if the plays had been 'sent before [their] time / Into this breathing world scarce half made up', as the hunchback Richard III says of himself (*Richard III*, 1.1.20–1). Rather, Wittgenstein appears to have had in mind what he characterized as a certain 'asymmetry' in Shakespeare's work – a refusal of Classical ideals of order and form. Comparing Shakespeare's plays to dreams, Wittgenstein writes that 'a dream is all wrong, absurd, composite, and yet at the same time it is completely right: put together in *this* strange way it makes an impression. Why? I don't know.' Like a dream, a Shakespeare play for Wittgenstein lacks rational luminosity, determinate meaning. From this point of view, his comments open up something important about the nature of Shakespeare's achievement and legacies. Insofar as a sketch is incomplete, waiting to be realized and worked up more fully, either by its creator or another, we may indeed feel that Shakespeare's writing requires imaginative encounter, a bodying forth onto stage, and careful thought. The plays often take the form of a debate or argument, requiring us as spectators or readers to choose. Whose side are we on: Hal's or Falstaff's? Prospero's or Caliban's? Antony's or Caesar's? And, just as frequently, rather than plumping for one position among such options, the plays are quite willing to *abstain* from choice – to develop and elaborate contrasts rather than close them down or smooth them over (often with large consequences – so Indira Ghose writes in the present volume that 'What is missing' in Shakespeare's plays 'is moral closure').

This is the Shakespearean quality that the poet John Keats famously identified as 'negative capability': the intellectually honourable refusal to decide between equally compelling, but incompatible, attitudes towards life. What Shakespeare will *not* give us is a simple monological account of the world – a single, unified way of thinking and feeling. The astonishing and restless variety of his oeuvre, as well as of individual plays, has long been recognized as fundamental to his artistic achievement. The nineteenth-century German writer and critic Otto Ludwig perceptively characterized Shakespeare's art as one of 'contrast' (think of the way Shakespeare engrafts apparently disparate materials – the boozy Porter and the murder in *Macbeth*; the bawdy Clown just moments before Cleopatra's suicide). Such a gallimaufry of contrasting moods – comedy and tragedy commingled – might appear to lack an overarching vision. It certainly lacks Classical perfection.

If Shakespeare's is an art of multiplicity and variety rather than of sameness – and this is a traditional way of valuing as well as of criticizing it – it is also, famously, an art of problems. Obscurities abound, keeping theatre practitioners, scholars and critics busy. Why does Hamlet delay? What motivates Iago? Why does Edgar (disguised as Poor Tom) not reveal himself at once to his blind father Gloucester? Why on earth does Leontes (in *The Winter's Tale*) suspect his chaste wife Hermione? How laudable, really, is Henry V? What happens to Lear's Fool? Why does Helena (in *All's Well That Ends Well*) dote on the awful Bertram? What (in *The Merchant of Venice*) is the cause of Antonio's mysterious sadness? How acceptable is it, as far as a happy ending is concerned, that Demetrius is not relieved of the magical love-juice that forces him to love Helena against his will in *A Midsummer Night's Dream*? How successful will the marriages, or intended marriages, be at the end of some of the comedies? And so on. Everywhere in Shakespeare we find gaps and openings, vaguenesses, aspects of the plays we struggle to make sense of, or that challenge closure and formal order. From the late nineteenth century critics were attracted to a sub-genre that became known as 'the problem play', a flexible category including such works as *Troilus and Cressida, Measure for Measure, All's Well That Ends Well, Timon of Athens* and even *Hamlet, Julius Caesar* and *Antony and Cleopatra*. In fact almost all of the plays are 'problematic' in some sense (how such problems are handled, if not solved, can be fully worked out by performance alone).

This indeterminacy – Wittgenstein's 'sketchiness' – is of the essence. The critic William Empson praised this Shakespearean quality in his *Seven Types of Ambiguity*, published in 1930, which valued complexity and difficulty rather than simplicity, resolution and closure. Shakespeare's ambiguities made him kin to the experimental writers, readers, artists and theatre practitioners of the twentieth century. As the novelist Javier Marías points out in these pages, so much of Shakespeare's language – *The Tempest*'s 'dark backward and abysm of time', for example (1.2.50) – defies logical explication. But these obscurities present opportunities to readers and spectators, to critics, writers, actors, directors, and filmmakers. It is the open-ended quality of much of Shakespeare's writing that spurs others' creativity.

That Shakespeare's plays are fruitfully indeterminate is related to a long-established claim that Shakespeare is somehow affiliated with, or impelled by, nature. The opening scene of *Timon of Athens* (understood to be by Shakespeare, with Thomas Middleton contributing the second scene of the first act) provides us with a brief yet imaginative piece of literary criticism. The character identified simply as 'Poet' depicts his work as a kind of natural process, devoid of conscious direction. Asked by a painter whether he is composing 'some work' for 'the great lord' Timon, the Poet rather disingenuously denies that his work has been prompted by desire for a patron's gold; instead, it is

> A thing slipp'd idly from me.
> Our poesy is as a gum which oozes
> From whence 'tis nourish'd; the fire i'th' flint
> Shows not till it be struck: our gentle flame
> Provokes itself, and like the current flies
> Each bound it chases.
>
> (1.1.20–5)

The 'gentle flame' of poetry is unlike the 'flint' in that it does not need to be 'struck' in order to leap into being. Rather than being a passive response to a stimulus (the need or desire to praise Timon, so that the Poet may be appropriately rewarded), poetry freely 'Provokes itself'. The passage is gently satirical: the Poet's work is of course motivated by desire for gain.

But what is interesting about this image of poetry as an oozy gum is that it pulls against Classical notions of completion, polish, and even conscious workmanship. The view is akin to Keats's conception that poetry should come as 'naturally' to a poet 'as the leaves to a tree'. For Shakespeare's Poet, then, poetry is non-volitional speech that requires little or no planning, control, or deliberation. Indeed, the 'oozing' itself suggests movement; what is being described here is an organic and unconscious process rather than any act of purposive design that leads to closure. This sense of something free of final form, natural, incomplete, spontaneous is nicely captured in Wittgenstein's use of the word 'sketch'. The Poet's characterization of poetry as an organic phenomenon is hugely suggestive in relation to Shakespeare. Because the plays have this problematic, mobile, unsettled or fugitive quality, such that they are never quite fully captured by the intellect, they can seem essentially natural rather than artificial – full of life and potential: as Tom Bishop writes in the present volume, Shakespeare's plays throng with 'leadings and potential realizations'.

The idea that Shakespeare is in a profound way associated with nature has been with us for so long it is hard to think of him otherwise. As Wittgenstein says elsewhere in his notes, 'people stare at [Shakespeare] in wonderment, almost as at a spectacular natural phenomenon'. He speculated that the capacity to 'admire' Shakespeare 'properly' might require being able 'to accept him as he is ... in the way you accept nature, a piece of scenery for example, just as it is'. Shakespeare was understood in this naturalistic way from the beginning. John Heminges and Henry Condell, responsible for assembling the First Folio of 1623, represent composition for Shakespeare as an unencumbered natural creative flow: 'his mind and hand went together, and what he thought he uttered with that easiness, that we have scarce received from him a blot in his papers'. Their comment conveys something essential about Shakespeare's style, its rapid, coalescent, nimble movement, one element merging swiftly and imperceptibly into another. The novelist Virginia Woolf was of a similar opinion, recording in her diary for 13 April 1930 that she preferred to read Shakespeare directly upon finishing her own writing, when her 'mind [was] agape and red-hot':

> Then it is astonishing. I never knew yet how amazing his stretch and speed and word coining power is, until I felt it utterly outpace and outrace my own, seeming to start equal and then I see him draw ahead and do things I could not in my wildest tumult and utmost press of mind imagine.

All of the great commentators have perceived this effortless, 'natural' quality of Shakespeare's writing – and how it can make other literature look artificial or made up. The idea that Shakespeare is himself a world, or nature – that there is a cosmic vastness about the works – is repeatedly encountered. John Dryden stressed Shakespeare's multi-dimensionality: 'he was the man who of all modern, and perhaps ancient poets, had the largest and most *comprehensive soul*'; Coleridge called him 'myriad-minded'. In Holy Trinity Church in Stratford, the funerary bust includes the words 'Shakespeare with whom / quick nature died', suggesting that part of Nature herself died when Shakespeare did. For John Milton, too, Shakespeare was the poet of nature.

Readers will find echoes of these sentiments among the reflections gathered in Part Two of this book. Such perceptions remind us how Shakespeare has been experienced *as a world* – not, that is, as someone who simply or passively depicts or copies the world, but who creates his own. These contributions by creative artists and practitioners from around the globe bring an unashamedly celebratory feeling to this collection. They range from early memories of Shakespeare at school (for example, Gregory Doran, the Artistic Director of The Royal Shakespeare Company, finding Shakespeare as a way out of being bullied), through to the political, psychological, theatrical, and theological perspectives of such voices as Ellen Geer, Lisa Wolpe, Debra Ann Byrd, Janet Suzman, Kenneth Branagh, Simon Russell Beale, Salley Vickers and Rowan Williams.

To identify Shakespeare with nature is to find in his works a generative or creative, rather than merely reflective, relation to reality. Art, at least Shakespeare's, does not simply 'hold … the mirror up to nature', as Hamlet had it (3.2.23); instead it *is* nature – is 'part of the res [that is, the thing or substance, reality] itself and not about it', in Wallace Stevens's phrase. If Shakespeare simply described what was already 'out there' it is hard to see how he could act as a stimulus to new creativity. By generating a new 'world' or 'nature', he augments our experience, which can then be drawn upon and inspire new creative endeavours. Encountering characters as vivid as Caliban, Lady Macbeth or Hamlet, or poetry of the order of that found in *Antony and Cleopatra* or *Othello*, is the kind of intense experience that itself becomes material for further art-making.

By giving us new experiences Shakespeare's works provide material for subsequent creative acts. Like other great artists, such as Chaucer (of whose *Canterbury Tales* Dryden declared 'Here is God's Plenty'), Shakespeare constitutes a realm of being. By creating a world that has the breadth, solidity and contradictoriness of actuality itself – one full of any number of contrasting experiences and feelings and points of view – Shakespeare's work makes itself available to others (for realization, extension, transformation, reconception), and with wonderful generosity. Polixenes's words in *The Winter's Tale* – 'The art itself is nature' – apply to Shakespeare himself; and help to explain why so many other artists have found in him material profoundly stimulating for their own art.

In what follows, a range of significant critics, writers and artists reflect upon the ways in which Shakespeare – this 'great creating nature' (*The Winter's Tale*, 4.4.88) – has shaped artistic invention in an astonishing range of forms and styles, from his own day to ours. Our sense of this volume is, that for each of our contributors, Shakespeare, like all great art, inspires a version of the following reaction: 'Yes; I sometimes feel like this too.' To experience that kind of response is to love the work of art, and to want to express love for it.

Part One

Essays

1

Shakespeare and the Theatre

Paul Prescott

R: *Do you think that all this and the rest of it can be read in the play?*
B: *Read in it and read into it.*
BERTOLT BRECHT, 'STUDY OF THE FIRST SCENE OF SHAKESPEARE'S *CORIOLANUS*', 1953

'Why don't you let them see Othello *instead?*'
'I've told you; it's old. Besides, they couldn't understand it.'
Yes, that was true. He remembered how Helmholtz had laughed at Romeo
and Juliet. *'Well then,' he said, after a pause, 'something new that's like*
Othello, *and that they could understand.'*
*'That's what we've all been wanting to write,' said Helmholtz, breaking a
long silence.*
ALDOUS HUXLEY, *BRAVE NEW WORLD*, 1932

Two Shakespearean negotiations of the past and the future: 1950s Soviet Berlin and London in the year AD 2540. The first epigraph offers a documentary insight into the creative process: Bertolt Brecht and a collaborator discussing the Berliner Ensemble's adaptation of *Coriolanus*. Brecht's colleague is vexed about fidelity and, specifically, whether the Ensemble's pro-plebeian version of *Coriolanus* is faithful to Shakespeare's original text. Brecht's response is only partly reassuring. The second, a fictional account of the problems of creative reproduction in the antiseptic future imagined in Huxley's *Brave New World*. Here the taste of the society has changed so much (has indeed been forcibly changed) that audiences are no longer equipped for, or sympathetic to, the tragic ethos of *Othello*. In both cases, something new is required: Shakespeare's legacy is both an obstacle and an opportunity. A creative solution needs to be grappled from two related problems. How do you make a Shakespeare play do and say what you want it to? How do you make something new, but something new that's *like* a Shakespeare play? These might be viewed as evolutionary problems, relating as they do to the impulse to adapt and make something fit in order for it to survive and the adaptor to prosper. 'Something new that's like *Othello*' – evolution is mutation; adaptation is repetition with a difference.

Over the last four centuries, Shakespeare's works have proved to be extremely 'adaptogenic' (a relatively recent word, but also one that Huxley might have invented) and nowhere have they been so creatively refashioned and reproduced as in their natural habitat, the theatre. Shakespeare's creative legacy to the theatre is to have left it a matchless collection of plays, a stupefyingly generous benefaction to the primary legatees, the theatre artists of the world. According to the *OED*, a legacy can be: 'A sum of money, or a specified article, given to another by will' (II.5a). As a so-called 'public good', Shakespeare's works are characterized by their non-excludability and non-rivalry in consumption. In other words, and unlike the resources bequeathed in most legacies or wills, his works can be consumed by all without being depleted. Perhaps the opposite is true: the more often Shakespeare's plays are used, the more they grow as a resource of creative capital in the world bank of culture.

Shakespeare didn't mention his works in the three pages that constitute his last will and testament. Part of his creative legacy is therefore not to have been explicit on the subject of what his works meant and how they should be performed. It is pleasant to think that, even if Shakespeare had written elaborate staging and set directions and a range of paratextual commentaries, he might nevertheless have taken the liberal and permissive attitude of a modern playwright like, for example, Peter Shaffer. Shaffer wrote in his Introduction to the revised version of *Amadeus* that, in publishing detailed stage directions based on the original production, 'it is no part of my desire to imprison the play in one particular presentation; still less to encourage the automatic borrowing of an original director's ideas by future interpreters. I hope that *Amadeus* will enjoy a vigorous life in many differing productions.'

Whether Shakespeare willed it or not, all of his plays have enjoyed varied and vigorous afterlives on the world's stages. Some of these productions have sought to be faithful to presumed authorial intention or to the original conditions of performance; more often theatre-makers have sought to please themselves and their audiences by fashioning the texts to speak to contemporary tastes and concerns, and by harnessing the latest theatrical technology to convey the story as spectacularly or sensually as possible. Whatever they think they're doing – whether reading *in* or reading *into*, presenting the 'authentic' *Othello* or 'something new that's like *Othello*' – all theatre-makers are engaged in an act of collaborative co-creation with Shakespeare's legacy. All of these acts create new works that are, as Sir Toby Belch might have it, 'consanguineous', blood-related to Shakespeare's texts; the family resemblance will sometimes be clear, sometimes remote.

What follows is a non-exhaustive lexicon of adaptive tactics that practitioners can and have used in response to Shakespeare's dramatic works. Most of these relate to the creative theatrical work of playwrights, actor-managers, dramaturges and directors. The creativity of the actor would require a different lexicon and the creative contributions (often crucial) of choreographers, composers, set and lighting designers, fight directors et al. would require a much more technical vocabulary. Most of the creative artists and works cited here are, for the curious, only a search-engine click away. (And while the presence of individual names might appear to support a romantic or heroic view of creativity, it is worth noting that nearly every individual here has depended on the industry and invention of others to realize their vision.) I have tried wherever possible to present the concept as an activity, process or action – something that people can and have done *to* and *with* Shakespeare's texts, or with the themes and ideas suggested by them. I hope this modest lexicon might even prove useful in inspiring (or purging) the temporarily 'blocked' creative artist faced with the task of making Shakespeare (or something new that's like Shakespeare) 400 years after the playwright's death.

***

Adaptation – a catch-all word for a piece of theatre modelled on or inspired by a work or works of Shakespeare. Etymologically: to fit to a new context (with

Darwinian under- and overtones). Much ink has been spilled in assessing the finer taxonomical distinctions between what counts as an adaptation, an offshoot, an appropriation, a spin-off, etc. Some argue (plausibly) that every production of a Shakespearean play – no matter how apparently 'faithful', straight or neutral – is in fact an adaptation, involving as it (usually) must cutting and other key interpretative choices relating to casting, scenography, direction, costume and the vast array of non-verbal meaning generated by any performance.

Animalization – the introduction of live (non-human) animals to charm, thrill, amuse or provoke philosophical reflection. Relatively rare. Shakespeare definitely calls for it once (the dog Crab in *The Two Gentlemen of Verona*), and some argue that the Bear that pursued Antigonus to his exit in the first performances of *The Winter's Tale* was a real example of the species. Creative examples in theatre after the early modern period include horses (typically in productions of Roman or English history plays), rabbits (Herbert Beerbohm Tree's 1900 *A Midsummer Night's Dream*), and the occasional non-venomous asp (*Antony and Cleopatra*). Writer and critic Henry Chance Newton (1854–1931) recalled 'several condensed versions of *Hamlet* in which we used a real dog star to work the *dénouement*'. 'F. R. Benson's idea of Caliban was to come on stage with a fish [presumably deceased] in his mouth' complained Edward Gordon Craig. *King Lear With Sheep* – a one-man, nine-ovine affair that handsomely delivers on its title – is playing in London at the time of writing.

Archaeological – an approach to staging Shakespeare in which the historical settings of the play's fictional locales are realized with elaborate accuracy. Especially popular in the nineteenth century or during any period undergoing a craze for classicism. Actor-manager Charles Kean (1811–68) was proud to list the affiliation 'F.S.A' (Fellow of the Society of Antiquaries) after his name. Often a form of super-sizing in which maximal human and non-human resources are thrown at the production in the hope of overwhelming – or simply outnumbering – the audience. But also a meme in the discourse of creativity; artists and critics alike are fond of metaphors drawn from archaeology and one will often find them mining the text's many layers, uncovering nuggets of gold or truth, brushing the dust off to reveal the original in all its pristine brilliance, etc.

Burlesque – from the Italian (*burla*) for mockery; a skittish, playful entertainment designed solely to amuse by undercutting the solemnity or pathos of the original. Usually though not exclusively based on Shakespeare's tragedies (including tragical histories such as *Richard III*); the gap between noble original and parodic adaptation, between high and low falutin', has historically proved entertaining. 'The sacrilegious hands of the parodist do not appear to have been laid on Shakespeare much before the end of the eighteenth century' noted R. Farquharson Sharp in 1920, before concluding, more in sorrow than in anger: 'the appeal of such things arises from their pandering to the low liking, which persists in human nature, for seeing solemn things made to look absurd'. The nineteenth century was one of the golden ages of Shakespearean burlesque or 'travestie' as it was more commonly known – witness such titles as: *King Lear and his Daughters Queer* (1830), *Macbeth Modernized; A Most Illegitimate Drama* (1838), *Hamlet the Ravin' Prince of Denmark; or, The Baltic Swell and the Diving Belle* (1866). The postmodern period (whenever that started) has also proved congenial to pastiche and parody; the Reduced Shakespeare Company's *The Complete Works of William Shakespeare (Abridged)* has played across the globe since 1987. History has so far corroborated George Bernard Shaw's opinion that 'Shakespeare will survive any possible extremity of caricature'.

Casting – arguably the most important act of theatre-making, all too often executed without creativity, imagination or risk. The stage must be peopled and what those people look and sound like, where they come from, and what they represent has implications for the audience experience, and for the reputation of Shakespeare within wider culture. In short: the question of who gets to speak Shakespeare is a political issue. Clichéd casting fulfils audience expectations and often results from unexamined conventions – we know from the text of *King Lear* that Cordelia is the youngest of the three daughters, but many productions will cast an actress that is a) blonde and b) apparently half the age of her older (darker haired) sisters, two choices for which there is scant justification in the text but which neatly pander to some regressive cultural assumptions. A casting equivalent of Mercutio's *punto reverso* can be achieved by presenting the audience with the opposite of what it might have expected or imagined: a geriatric Romeo and Juliet in Ben Power's collage piece *A Tender Thing* (2009); a matriarchal monarch in Ellen Geer's selectively gender-bending *Queen Lear* (2014); a monoglot white American Othello (Bill Pullman) surrounded by bilingual (English and Norwegian) Venetians, as in Stein Winge's 2015 production in Bergen. In the words of Leah Adcock-Starr, the director of an all-female 2015 *Hamlet* in Minneapolis: 'Good Stories belong to everyone. Is Hamlet a woman's story? Yes? No? It's a Good Story [...] Sometimes it may take a re-framing (like an all-female cast) to unearth and explore the ways in which stories we think we know and believe might be about or belong to someone else, might in fact, be more ours than we first imagined.'

Collage – a term borrowed from the visual arts where it describes the arrangement of various objects in a delimited space. Theatre is a temporal as well as spatial art form, so the analogy isn't exact, but this term generally stands for an adaptation that has cut, rearranged and reassigned lines, as well as disrupted the order of scenes and speeches as found in the original. A quick route to defamiliarization. In relation to Shakespearean creativity, the term is synonymous with Charles Marowitz whose 'Collages' based on *Hamlet*, *Macbeth* and *Othello* opened the way, as he saw it, for 'zillions of interpretations of the collected works [and] countless new permutations of the plays themselves; configurations never dreamt of in Shakespeare's philosophy, or anyone else's'. See also Djanet Sears's *Harlem Duet* (1997) that creates a collage-like exploration of *Othello*, race and American history by switching between timeframes and between fiction and non-fiction.

Copyright – the enemy of creativity (cf. the limpet grip exerted by the Samuel Beckett estate on productions of works by that playwright). Magnificently irrelevant in the case of Shakespeare, where artists and writers are freely able to reproduce with a difference, or copywrong. In the 1980s Prince Philip suggested that American theatre companies should pay a levy every time they performed Shakespeare to help fund the building of Shakespeare's Globe in London, but the plan came to nought and the public recitation of Shakespeare's words in America, as throughout the world, remains unregulated and untaxed.

Cutting – the removal of lines or scenes in the interests of clarity, accessibility, taste or train timetables. Viewed by a puritanical minority as intrinsically suspicious, although the process clearly dates from Shakespeare's own time. And given that 'only a maniac is never bored in the theatre' (Kenneth Tynan) and that 'even the Sermon on the Mount could use some cutting' (Tyrone Guthrie), it follows that only bore-proof fundamentalists truly relish every syllable of an uncut performance. An aversion to cutting can lead to the acquisition of a nickname, as it did in the case of William Bridges-Adams, the director of the Shakespeare Memorial Theatre from 1919–34, known to weary punters as 'Unabridges-Adams'. Reviewing productions from which their favourite line has been excised, waggish critics are apt to declare 'this was the unkindest cut of all'.

Decentring – the act of refocusing the play away from its customary centre; not necessarily *Hamlet* without the Prince, but certainly *Hamlet* in which the Prince is not the main object of attention. Prime example: Tom Stoppard's *Rosencrantz and Guildenstern Are Dead* (1966), in which the hapless pair take centre stage (and which is also an adaptation of *Waiting for Godot* that somehow evaded copyright fees from the Beckett estate). Decentred adaptations often seek to redress a political imbalance by focusing on underwritten characters, as in the (very different) examples of Paula Vogel's *Desdemona: A Play about a Handkerchief* (1993), Toni Morrison's *Desdemona* (2011) and Howard Barker's *Gertrude – The Cry* (2002). In otherwise 'straight' productions, decentring can sometimes happen by accident: Kenneth Tynan wrote of a 1953 Stratford-upon-Avon production that *Richard III* is 'generally regarded as a one-man show' but that in this rendering 'the man in question was the Duke of Buckingham'; this was presumably not what the director or the actor playing Richard intended.

Domestification – also known as indigenization – producing Shakespeare's plays in such a way that they feel, sound or look familiar and recognizable to a specific audience. This might be a case of drawing on indigenous performance traditions, conventions and styles or of placing the play at a specific moment that resonates with the audience and allows them to make sense of the text in the light of their pre-existing historical knowledge. Yukio Ninagawa's 2015 *Hamlet* (the director's eighth distinct production of the play) featured both modes of domestification: the setting was a poor urban neighbourhood in late-nineteenth-century Japan (the cultural moment when *Hamlet* first played in the country), while the play-within-the-play was presented in a formal manner reminiscent of Kabuki theatre. Domestification often produces or is inspired by topicality: Sulayman Al-Bassam's *The Al-Hamlet Summit* (2002) transplanted Shakespeare's play into the contemporary Middle East to create a political tragedy of regime change, petro-dollars and arms deals, while the riotous opening of Nuno Cardoso's 2014 production of *Coriolanus* in Lisbon clearly alluded to recent anti-austerity demonstrations in that city.

Downsizing – producing Shakespeare with fewer resources than obtained in original performances and/or are found in standard contemporary mainstream productions. Characterized by inexpensive costuming, minimal sets and scenery, and small casts. Can stem from economic necessity, aesthetic preference or both. Inventive doubling, trebling, quadrupling can draw attention to patterning across the play, creating echoes unimagined by the author, as well as generating audience pleasure at the actor's art and labour. Many directors and creative teams (including e.g. Deborah Warner or Cheek by Jowl) have at least begun their careers touring a small cast in the back of a van around village halls and leisure centres. One of the most enjoyable shows in the history of Shakespeare's Globe to date was Mike Alfreds's pared-back and downsized 2001 production of *Cymbeline* presented with six actors in a default outfit of off-white pyjamas.

Extraction – creating a new piece of theatre by detaching character(s) or scene(s) from their plays. This might form a monodrama – e.g. Tim Crouch's series of one-man shows: *I, Peaseblossom*; *I, Cinna*; *I, Malvolio*; et al. – or a stand-alone entertainment (e.g. the so-called 'droll' entitled *The Grave-Makers* [c. 1650], based on 5.1 of *Hamlet*, or the Beatles' rendition of *Pyramus and Thisbe* broadcast on UK TV to celebrate Shakespeare's 400th birthday in 1964). As I write, Frank Bramwell's *King Lear (Alone)* is playing at the Buxton

Fringe Festival, a post-scripting concerned with Lear's 'spiritual journey following the news of Cordelia's death'. Bramwell speaks for many fans of extraction when he claims: 'By losing the other twenty-nine characters of the original play, this allows us to get inside the very thought and feelings of King Lear himself.' As here, extractions are often based on the assumption that characters have selves beyond their existence as a series of speech acts in Shakespeare's plays.

Framing – situating the performance of a Shakespeare play within a specific historical moment or cultural space so that it becomes, in effect, a play-within-a-play. There is at least half a precedent for this in Shakespeare: *The Taming of the Shrew* begins with a lengthy Induction but the text that survives, for whatever reason, fails to return us to the framing world at the play's conclusion. Framing spaces have included schools (Joe Calarco's *Shakespeare's R+J* [1998]) or prisons (Phyllida Lloyd's female-prison-set *Julius Caesar* [2012] and *Henry IV, 1* [2014] at the Donmar Warehouse). Other notable 'framed' productions include: George Tabori's 1966 *The Merchant of Venice as Performed in Theresienstadt*, in which Jewish prisoners performed the play for Nazi guards, and – more recently and in a different key entirely – Chris Abraham's production of *A Midsummer Night's Dream* (Stratford Festival, Canada, 2014) which opened with a garden party celebrating a same-sex marriage (a nod to the theory that this work was originally intended as a wedding-play) and proceeded, with riotous invention, ostensibly to improvise a performance of the text drawing on the guests attending (and props typically found at) the wedding reception.

Fumigation – the process of deodorizing Shakespeare on the grounds of moral and/or aesthetic indecency. Henry Irving (1838–1905), for example, thought that *Troilus and Cressida* could not be put before his audience without extensive fumigation. Neo-Classical Stuarts and Georgians, squeamish Victorians, and proper Edwardians (i.e., most periods in British history) have left us plenty of entertaining examples of queasy bowdlerization. But before we in the present get too swollen with 'the enormous condescension of posterity' (in E. P. Thompson's phrase), it is worth noting that it is common for present-day Anglophone performances silently to fumigate any offhand reference that might lead to the impression that Shakespeare was a racist or an anti-Semite. It is currently rare to hear any Benedick say of his Beatrice 'If I do not love her, I am a Jew' (*Much Ado About Nothing*, 2.3.252–3), or for Lance to demonstrate his dog's hard-heartedness by comparing it to an almost equally hard-hearted, generic Jew (*The Two Gentlemen of Verona*, 2.3.10–1).

A commonly cited landmark in the history of censorship is the unlamented demise of the Lord Chamberlain in 1968, after whose departure actors disrobed en masse in raunchy shows such as John Barton's 1968 RSC *Troilus and Cressida*, a production that prompted at least one spectator (Lieutenant Colonel L. C. Gayer) to write to the *Daily Telegraph* complaining that 'Mr Barton has taken the liberty of introducing a highly sensational drunken homosexual orgy scene with no justification whatever'. It is not at all uncommon for contemporary (especially continental European) productions to treat audiences to what Lt. Col. Gayer and other fumigators would describe as 'four or five minutes of irrelevant unpleasantness'.

Identification – every reader or viewer of a play finds their own moments of heightened engagement, empathy and rapport with Shakespeare's works, whether through alignment with specific characters, or ideas, or combinations of words. Identification is at the centre of many actors' creative process (and, in turn, of the audience's response to their performance). Laurence Olivier realized he had to love Richard III in order to play him and audiences loved his Richard accordingly. The approach was formalized by Stanislavski and elaborated by, e.g., Strasberg in the 'Method', but the quest to identify with the character has surely been central to the actor's art since at least Shakespeare's time. The creative act is engaged by the 'Magic If' – an ethical identification that Shakespeare stages in such memorable set-pieces as Sir Thomas More's defence of refugees and Emilia's of wronged wives. It is also the case that adaptors usually feel an elective affinity with the text they are adapting, although this can sometimes be provoked by a kind of negative identification whereby irritation or anger with the Shakespearean text provokes an aggressive rewriting.

Imitation – wanting to write like Shakespeare – an understandable wish and the highest form of flattery but not always guaranteed to yield the desired results. If not careful, can shade into inadvertent burlesque or the merely pedestrian or soporific. As Samuel Johnson pointed out: 'Almost all absurdity of conduct arises from the imitation of those we cannot resemble.' Examples: the unreadable and unstageable slew of pseudo-Shakespearean plays written in the nineteenth century; John Keats's fragment *King Stephen* (1819) is perhaps an honourable exception. More egregiously, imitations have been passed off as originals, as in the remarkable attempted forgery perpetrated on 1790s London by Samuel and William Henry Ireland. See also the fascinating case of the French playwright Jean-François Ducis (1733–1816), whose 'imitations' of Shakespeare spread across Europe in multiple new translations – often the first in that particular language – despite the fact that Ducis had written his 'imitations' without being able to read any English. No one knows quite how he pulled this off, but one sardonic contemporary, noting both Ducis's idolatrous veneration of Shakespeare and his ignorance of the English language, likened him to 'a priest without Latin'. For a successful imitation by an author who *could* read Shakespeare in English, see Pushkin's *Boris Godunov* (1825) with its unmistakable echoes of *Macbeth* and *Richard III*. Pushkin wrote that 'I imitated Shakespeare in his free and broad portrayal of characters, [and] in his careless and simple formation of plots' – imitation as liberation.

Improvement – the implicit goal of much creative engagement with Shakespeare. Few confess this for fear of seeming arrogant or hubristic, and tend to smuggle their 'improvements' in, just as John Barton did when he silently inserted hundreds of his own lines into his adaptation of the history plays (*The Wars of the Roses*, RSC, 1963). Others are unabashed. 'Throughout the fabric of his work', wrote the critic Max Beerbohm in 1901, 'you will find much that is tawdry, irrational, otiose – much that is, however shy you may be of admitting that it is, tedious'. The creative artist then has two options: to cut or to improve. George Bernard Shaw, Beerbohm's predecessor as reviewer on *The Saturday Review*, had an entertainingly ambivalent relationship to Shakespeare; on his more rancorous days, Shakespeare's 'legacy' carried for Shaw something of the technical meaning the word currently enjoys among computing experts: 'Designating software or hardware which, although outdated or limiting, is an integral part of a computer system and difficult to replace.' Shaw did his best, though, not least in his *Cymbeline Refinished* (1936), which attempted to improve the final act of that play by severe cutting and by rationalizing the number of revelations; without such improvements, Shaw felt, the act was merely 'a tedious string of unsurprising *dénouements* sugared with insincere sentimentality after a ludicrous stage battle'. As Shaw pointed out in the same preface, there has also been a long tradition of improving the ends of Shakespeare's plays by 'supplying them with what are called happy endings', a practice that has 'always been accepted without protest by British audiences'.

Improvisation – the intentional or accidental use of Shakespeare's words or scenarios as springboards for new flights of fancy and invention. Despite Hamlet's haughty and presumptuous 'advice' to the clowns to speak no more than is set down for them, audiences have enjoyed those moments (precious because usually rare) when actors go off-script; many of the best anecdotes from theatre history consist of a split-second moment of improvisation. More systematically, improvisation is a process that channels the sometimes aleatoric creativity of the actor in rehearsal and makes it integral to the interpretative process: Herbert Blau and his actors improvised within and around the text of *Hamlet* for a year (1975–6) before presenting the freely adaptive *Elsinore*.

Interculturalization – a cumbersome nonce word for an interesting phenomenon: the unleashing or creation of new meanings and dynamics by casting or setting productions in cultural contexts unknown to Shakespeare and his contemporaries. Opinion differs as to the extent of the mono- or multiculturalism of Elizabethan and Jacobean London, but we do know that every member of Shakespeare's acting company was a white, European male, many of whom would have been dependent on costume, appendages and make-up to impersonate men of other cultures and the female sex in general. While some directors and companies continue to pursue these mono-cultural (and, sometimes, mono-sexual) casting practices, others are more interested in what happens when the stage becomes a meeting-ground for actors and artists from a range of cultural and national backgrounds. The German director Karen Beier has staged *A Midsummer's Night Dream* (1995) and *The Tempest* (1997) with actors from across Europe and Israel, mostly speaking their native languages. In Beier's *Dream*, rehearsals for *Pyramus and Thisbe* consisted of an informal intercultural acting competition between proponents of different acting styles. At the time of writing, UK director Tim Supple has just embarked on a two-year project that pulls actors from all over the world into a polyglot and experimental *King Lear*, just as his earlier production of *A Midsummer Night's Dream* (2006) featured actors from all over the Indian subcontinent in a multilingual text.

Mashing up – The compound word 'mash-up' was rare before the late-twentieth century, since when it has been widely used to describe a piece of music created by merging the elements of two or more existing songs or tracks. But the technique can be seen in early theatre adaptations such as William Davenant's *The Law Against Lovers* (1662), a mash-up of *Much Ado* and *Measure for Measure* and Thomas Otway's *The History and Fall of Caius Marius* (1679), an equally unlikely but intriguing combination of *Coriolanus* and *Romeo and Juliet*. More recently, the mash-up has become a staple technique of 'fan-fiction' and is therefore perhaps more common in novels and short stories than on stage, although a play such as Ann-Marie MacDonald's *Goodnight Desdemona (Good Morning Juliet)* (1988) inserts its modern-day heroine into the fictional worlds of both *Othello* and *Romeo and Juliet*.

Modernization – the rational assumption that contemporary audiences might enjoy a rendition of Shakespeare that looks and sounds like the present. A specific form of domestification. Modernization is primarily conveyed visually, and some element of modern-dress costuming has featured in Shakespearean production from Shakespeare's day to the present. It has been increasingly common since early pioneers like Barry Jackson, whose series of three modern-dress productions at Birmingham Rep in the 1920s (*Cymbeline*, 1923; *Hamlet*, 1925; *Macbeth*, 1928) insisted on presenting Shakespeare as his audience's contemporary. The choice of contemporary settings often invites theatre-makers to rethink issues relating to politics and casting. Iqbal Khan's 2015 *Othello* at the RSC not only cast a black actor (Lucian Msamati) as Iago, it also situated the action of the play in a multicultural context that may have said little about race in Shakespeare's England but made exciting sense of the complex dynamics of modern race and racism in the UK. Modernization is generally easier in non-Anglophone countries where productions will often commission new translations that capture the tang and slang of contemporary speech.

Musicalization – the introduction of music where it is not explicitly called for in the text, or the wholesale musicalization of Shakespeare's plays. All art, Walter Pater averred, aspires to the condition of music; many contemporary productions of Shakespeare aspire to the condition of The Musical. This is an honourable tradition stretching back to such notable adaptations as Thomas Shadwell's 1674 operatic *Tempest*. Garrick's version of a musical adaptation of *Pyramus and Thisbe* advertised itself: 'Where *Shakespear* has not supplied the Composer with Songs, he has taken from *Milton, Waller, Dryden, Hammond &c.* and it is hoped they will not seem unnaturally introduced', a hope shared by many theatrical producers before and since. For some, Cole Porter's *Kiss Me, Kate* (1948) and Bernstein and Sondheim's *West Side Story* (1957) are, as works of art, distinct improvements on the Shakespearean originals on which they are based.

Post-scripting – a creative response to the widespread sense that the conclusions of Shakespeare's plays often feature loose ends and unfinished business, or else fail to satisfy. This process began within Shakespeare's lifetime – John Fletcher's *The Tamer Tam'd* (1611) is a sequel to *The Taming of the Shrew* in which, as Fletcher's title hints, Petruchio gets a dose of his own medicine from the woman he marries after his first wife, Kate, has died. David Greig's *Dunsinane* (2010), in which Lady Macbeth has survived ('the Queen, my lord, is not dead'), and is pursuing her claim to the throne, is a twenty-first-century example.

***

Postscript: What is clear from this far-from-complete lexicon is that Shakespearean theatrical creativity is by definition collaborative and co-dependent. Isaac Asimov, reflecting on the fact that Alfred Wallace and Charles Darwin had developed their own theories of evolution at the same time through a similar route, noted that creative thinking often consisted of the ability to make connections: 'what is needed is not only people with a good background in a particular field, but also people capable of making a connection between item 1 and item 2 which might not ordinarily seem connected.' Applied to Shakespeare's creative legacy, item 1 is 'Shakespeare', but item 2 can be *anything*. And however we define 'creativity' – as divergent or flexible thinking, fluid intelligence or conceptual blending – at its best it will involve some kind of combination of item 1 and item 2 into something new that's like Shakespeare.

2

Shakespeare and Poetry

Sukanta Chaudhuri

Shakespeare wrote two long narrative poems, 154 sonnets, and a sprinkling of other short poems. They amount to hardly 5 per cent of his works, the rest being plays. Yet Shakespeare is called a poet more often than a dramatist. The plays, moreover, are poetic dramas: their language is the language of poetry. Vastly more people across the world have read them than seen them acted. Both of his non-dramatic long poems end in death; but while *The Rape of Lucrece* strikes a sombre note of tragedy and state affairs, *Venus and Adonis* is mythic and romantic, with potential material for comedy. Both poems mesh with the language of Shakespeare's earlier drama, while the complex human relationships in the *Sonnets* also look forward to the later plays. In fact, Shakespeare's crucial achievement is a new integration of poetic language with dramatic action and character.

The general development of poetic language is perhaps his most far-reaching legacy. In the poetry of later times, it operates at several levels, which I will take up in turn at each stage of my account. The most obvious level comprises explicit references to Shakespearean works and characters. Next come quotations and echoes. Beyond these lies a subtler stylistic influence, harder to prove but often clearly discernible to the ear when read aloud. More fundamentally still, Shakespeare's language can make other poets think about their own. None of these effects is confined to English literary history, though of course that is where they appear earliest and most sustainedly. They penetrate many languages in many guises, extending the material of his poetic drama into non-dramatic contexts.

This took some time to happen. The late seventeenth and eighteenth centuries favoured a more formal, Classical style than Shakespeare's. He was seen as 'Fancy's child' (in John Milton's phrase, from his poem 'L'Allegro'), practising a simpler, more artless poetry. His plays were commonly acted in elaborate reworkings where his own lines were overshadowed. The eighteenth century, the first great age of Shakespeare scholarship, did not uniformly admire his verse. Alexander Pope and Samuel Johnson (like John Dryden before them) criticize what they see as his verbosity and bombast. But Johnson also praises him for a quality shared with Edmund Spenser, 'smoothness and harmony'.

Such praise accords with one of Shakespeare's most accessible veins: a smooth, lyrical but delicately varied flow, embellished by simple yet subtle images:

> Your eyes are lode-stars, and your tongue's sweet air
> More tuneable than lark to shepherd's ear,
> When wheat is green, when hawthorn buds appear.
>
> (*A Midsummer Night's Dream*, 1.1.183–5)

or,

> O swear not by the moon, th'inconstant moon,
> That monthly changes in her circled orb ...
>
> (*Romeo and Juliet*, 2.2.109–10)

As Shakespeare matures, his poetic luxuriance is increasingly tempered by the dramatic action and the speaker's character. This can be seen in Othello's

> Keep up your bright swords, for the dew will rust them.
>
> (*Othello*, 1.2.59)

or, in *The Tempest*, in Caliban's

> Pray you tread softly, that the blind mole may
> Not hear a footfall.
>
> (4.1.194–5)

The last passage impressed Johnson's younger contemporary Joseph Warton as 'highly poetical'. Warton's taste prefigured that of the Romantics of the next century. 'He has a magic power over words,' says William Hazlitt of

Shakespeare: 'they come winged at his bidding'. Samuel Taylor Coleridge praises his 'deep feeling and exquisite sense of beauty', as conveyed through his control of form and his 'sweet and appropriate melody'. Championing as they did notions of poetic inspiration, the Romantics adopted Shakespeare's lyric strain, sometimes applied to Shakespearean material as in Shelley's 'With a Guitar, to Jane'. The poet as Ariel, spirit and servant of the magician Prospero in *The Tempest*, addresses his recipient as Miranda, Prospero's daughter:

> For by permission and command
> Of thine own Prince Ferdinand,
> Poor Ariel sends this silent token
> Of more than ever can be spoken;
> From Prospero's enchanted cell,
> As the mighty verses tell,
> To the throne of Naples, he
> Lit you o'er the trackless sea.

Such limpid verse owes more to the Elizabethan lyric generally than to Shakespeare. The latter provides more complex models.

It is not always easy to trace the imprint of earlier writing on a later literary idiom, but Shakespeare's presence in Romantic poetry is too prominent to miss. Even the Miltonic Wordsworth can strike a Shakespearean note. His address to his sister Dorothy in the 1798 poem 'Lines Written a Few Miles Above Tintern Abbey' expands, in Romantic vein, Caesar's to *his* sister Octavia in *Antony and Cleopatra* ('The elements be kind to thee, and make / Thy spirits all of comfort!', 3.2.40–1):

> Therefore let the moon
> Shine on thee in thy solitary walk;
> And let the misty mountain-winds be free
> To blow against thee: …
>   … thy mind
> Shall be a mansion for all lovely forms,
> Thy memory be as a dwelling place
> For all sweet sounds and harmonies …

There is the same wish for the sister's serenity of mind, expanded and openly philosophized in Wordsworth. Even the interaction with nature is anticipated in Caesar's reference to 'the elements'.

Shelley's poetry is steeped in Shakespeare. Lines from *Julius Caesar* (4.3.68–9) and *Measure for Measure* (2.2.118–19) combine in his 'philosophical poem' *Queen Mab*:

> Man's brief and frail authority
> Is powerless as the wind
> That passeth idly by.

In Shelley's lyrical drama *Prometheus Unbound*, Prometheus wants to retreat with Asia to a cave

> Where we will sit and talk of time and change,
> As the world ebbs and flows, ourselves unchanged.

Just so did the defeated King Lear envisage life in prison with Cordelia: they would live 'alone … like birds i'the cage', observing 'Who loses and who wins, who's in, who's out', while they 'wear out / … packs and sects of great ones / That ebb and flow by the moon' (5.3.9–19).

In 'Adonais', too, the 'Actaeon-like' Shelley's 'own thoughts' pursue him 'like raging hounds', repeating an image from *Twelfth Night* (1.1.21–3). Much deeper down, snatches from the scene of Imogen's supposed death in Shakespeare's *Cymbeline* (4.2.196–290) are worked into the lines of this elegy on John Keats's untimely death:

> Thy extreme hope, the loveliest and the last,
> The bloom, whose petals nipped before they blew
> Died on the promise of the fruit, is waste;
> The broken lily lies – the storm is overpast.

Likewise, in *Cymbeline*, Imogen is mourned as the 'sweetest, fairest lily' (4.2.201), followed by an image of 'flowers, now wither'd' (286). Flower-imagery, against a vivid backdrop of the seasonal cycle, permeates Shakespeare's scene and Shelley's poem. More basically, Shelley elaborates on the simple lyrical lament in *Cymbeline* for 'Golden lads and girls' now 'come to dust' (4.2.258–81).

Keats himself, whom Shelley mourns in 'Adonais', is accounted closest to Shakespeare in sensibility, most attuned to the older poet's language. He devises quintessentially Shakespearean compounds, even multiple compounds. 'Faint fare-thee-wells and sigh-shrilled adieus' in his *Endymion* strikes exactly the note of Shakespeare's 'world-without-end bargain' in *Love's Labour's Lost*, or 'all-too-precious you' in Sonnet 86. Edgar's words in *King Lear* to his blinded father Gloucester ('Hark, do you hear the sea?', 4.6.4), slightly misremembered, 'haunted' Keats so 'intensely' as to inspire a whole sonnet. Edgar had called a non-existent sea into being by words alone (4.6.11–24). That evocative description becomes Keats's cue to recreate the actual sea:

> It keeps eternal whisperings around
> Desolate shores, and with its mighty swell
> Gluts twice ten thousand caverns; till the spell
> Of Hecate leaves them their old shadowy sound.
>
> ('On the Sea')

Discussing the Shakespearean actor Edmund Kean, Keats writes: 'A melodious passage in poetry is full of pleasures both sensual and spiritual ... The sensual life of verse springs warm from the lips of Kean.' The phrasing conveys Keats's own full-bodied savouring of Shakespeare's language. Such sensuous utterance augments the 'spiritual' element, meaning not the religious or moral but the conceptual as embodied in imagery, what Keats called 'the hieroglyphics of beauty'. Keats's early poem *Sleep and Poetry* echoes Shakespeare's free-flowing yet dramatically-pointed verse:

> Stop and consider! Life is but a day;
> A fragile dewdrop on its perilous way
> From a tree's summit; a poor Indian's sleep
> While his boat hastens to the monstrous steep
> Of Montmorenci.

This is in Shakespeare's characteristic vein of lyric meditation, underpinned by images both from the enrichment of familiar experience and from remoter picturings. The 'poor Indian' recalls Othello's 'base Indian' ignorant of his own good (5.2.347). There are passages of more heightened, emotive rhetoric as well:

> An ocean dim, sprinkled with many an isle,
> Spreads awfully before me. How much toil!
> How many days! what desperate turmoil,
> Ere I can have explored its widenesses.
> Ah, what a task! upon my bended knees
> I could unsay those – no, impossible!
> Impossible!

In their broad dramatic movement, these lines can be compared to Prince Hal's reflections on the crown he removes from his dying father's bedside (*King Henry IV*, Part 2, 4.5.20–46), or the exchanges between Hamlet and his father's ghost (1.5.74–109), or Othello's farewell to happiness (3.3.348–60), among many possible analogues.

Keats works the whole spectrum of Shakespeare's verse. Vignettes from *Endymion* recall the *Sonnets* or early comedies: 'the poppies hung / Dew-dabbled on their stalks, the ouzel sung / A heavy ditty'. This recalls the vein I illustrated at the outset from *A Midsummer Night's Dream* and *Romeo and Juliet*. More intricate, cogitative passages, such as the following from Book One, recall the dark comedies and the tragedies:

> Life's self is nourished by its proper pith,
> And we are nurtured like a pelican brood.
> Aye, so delicious is the unsating food
> That men, who might have towered in the van
> Of all the congregated world, to fan
> And winnow from the coming step of time
> All chaff of custom, wipe away all slime
> Left by men-slugs and human serpentry,
> Have been content to let occasion die,
> Whilst they did sleep in love's elysium.

The tone and movement match Ulysses' half-satiric, half-meditative engagement with Achilles in Act 3, Scene 3 of *Troilus and Cressida*; or snatches from the sombre *Measure for Measure* (like 1.2.120–30 or 3.1.5–41); or Iago's cynic meditations in *Othello* (for example, 1.1.40–64, 3.3.135–64, or even the prose

1.3.321–34). Remarkably, Keats achieves these effects using couplets in iambic pentameter: the same line-length as Shakespeare's blank verse but with a radically different movement.

Alfred, Lord Tennyson inherited Shakespeare's lyricism, and Robert Browning his tougher figurative practice. This helped them each to develop a notable poetic form: one transformed since the sixteenth century, the other quite new. Tennyson's *In Memoriam* crowns many Victorian lyric sequences exploring deep personal relationships, exemplified for all time in Shakespeare's *Sonnets* and, more generally, in the genre of the Renaissance sonnet cycle. What is remarkable about *In Memoriam* is the way the poet's relationship with the dead Arthur Hallam renders in reverse, like a photographic negative, Shakespeare's with his living friend. Like the friend's 'eternal summer' in Sonnet 18, the 'dusk' of Hallam's death is unchanged by 'branding summer suns' (*In Memoriam*, II). Class and circumstance induced Shakespeare's distance from his friend. He might have said of the latter, for different reasons, what Tennyson says of Hallam:

> It was but unity of place
> That made me dream I rank'd with him.
>
> (XLII)

Yet Shakespeare's 'slight Muse' is thereby exalted to 'give / That due to thee which thou deserv'st alone' (Sonnets 38, 39). So does Tennyson's 'earthly Muse … darken … sanctities with song' by imbibing the words of 'the dear one dead' (XXXVII). Tennyson wants Hallam to be near him when his 'light is low' (L), just as Shakespeare, sunk in loss and grief, revives at the thought of his friend (Sonnets 29 and 30). Such parallels are always inconclusive. But Tennyson's un-Shakespearean philosophizing is underpinned by a human narrative that, while switching the context from life to death, reflects the course of the *Sonnets*.

The dramatic monologue, which Browning made his own, is fundamentally indebted to Shakespearean strategies of expressing character through language. Only one major instance, his 'Caliban upon Setebos', derives directly from Shakespeare. But the verse spoken by his Fra Lippo Lippi is akin in spirit to Falstaff's inspired prose, and Bishop Blougram's accents are like a genial retake of Ulysses' in *Troilus*. Most importantly, Browning alone among the great Victorians follows the turns and twists of introspective utterance, the sparks emitted as the mind forms its thoughts, that later endeared Shakespeare to the Modernists.

The nineteenth century was generally attentive to Shakespeare's imagery, where intellection becomes poetry. In 1837, the Spanish Shakespeare translator Joseph Blanco White (José María Blanco Crespo) observed that Shakespeare's metaphors 'are full of the truest and most rigorous Life. He shows you the secret ties of Relationship by which Nature connects the, apparently, most distant notions.' Coleridge and Keats would have agreed. But after Browning, the knottier aspects of Shakespeare's imagery, with the robust rhythms enshrining them, came to be newly valued in the next century.

Modernist poets could draw directly on the plays. In his *Last Poems*, Yeats credits certain Shakespearean heroes with a Romantic frenzy:

> Myself must I remake
> Till I am Timon and Lear
> Or that William Blake
> Who beat upon the wall
> Till Truth obeyed his call.
>
> ('An Acre of Grass')

A more introspective image of Lear may be implicit in

> Infirm and aged I might stay
> In some good company,
> I who have always hated work,
> Smiling at the sea …
>
> ('Are you content?')

and still more improbably, an introspective Timon in

> Why do I hate man, woman or event?
> That is a light my jealous soul has sent.
> From terror and deception freed it can
> Discover impurities, can show at last
> How soul may walk when all such things are past …
>
> ('Ribh considers Christian love insufficient')

This reflects the bleak withdrawal of spirit marking the last phase of Timon's misanthropy:

> My long sickness
> Of health and living now begins to mend,
> And nothing brings me all things.
>
> (*Timon of Athens*, 5.1.186–8)

T. S. Eliot, too, uses Shakespeare's characters as images and presences, metaphors rather than actual individuals: from the early Prufrock ('No! I am not Prince Hamlet') to the late unfinished sequence of poems 'Coriolan' ('That is all we could see. But how many eagles! and how many trumpets!'). A haunting Marina, new-found daughter of Pericles, symbolizes a revival of the spirit in 'Marina':

> This form, this face, this life
> Living to live in a world of time beyond me; let me
> Resign my life for this life, my speech for that unspoken,
> The awakened, lips parted, the hope, the new ships.

More extensively, in *The Sea and the Mirror,* his long poem based on *The Tempest*, W. H. Auden makes Shakespeare's characters sing like moderns and yet like themselves, from Miranda –

> He kissed me awake, and no one was sorry;
> The sun shone on sails, eyes, pebbles, anything,
> And the high green hill sits always by the sea.

– to the ship's master and boatswain:

> At Dirty Dick's and Sloppy Joe's
> We drank our liquor straight,
> Some went upstairs with Margery,
> And some, alas, with Kate.

Stephano and Trinculo might have sung this song.

For his remote successors, Shakespeare's men and women do not simply speak poetry but become the substance of poetry. Alongside these specific reworkings, there is again a wider, more elusive recourse to new resources of Shakespeare's language. The most untypical of Victorian poets was Gerard Manley Hopkins. His works appeared only in 1918, when English Modernism was stirring in Eliot, Ezra Pound, and others. In search of a new, rugged, challenging idiom, they unearthed a new Shakespeare as a model:

> Bloody, bawdy villain!
> Remorseless, treacherous, lecherous, kindless villain!
>
> *(Hamlet,* 2.2.582–3)

> If it were done, when 'tis done, then 'twere well
> It were done quickly.
>
> *(Macbeth,* 1.7.1–2)

These examples were cited by the critic F. R. Leavis, an early ideologue of English Modernism. Against them we can set a sonnet by Hopkins ('No worst, there is none') –

> O the mind, mind has mountains; cliffs of fall
> Frightful, sheer, no-man-fathomed. Hold them cheap
> May who ne'er hung there. Nor does long our small
> Durance deal with that steep or deep.

– or Pound in *Hugh Selwyn Mauberley* on the dead in the Great War:

> Died some, pro patria,
>   non 'dulce' non 'et decor' ...
> walked eye-deep in hell
> believing in old men's lies, then unbelieving
> came home, home to a lie ...

There is nothing directly Shakespearean here, but the turns and pauses in Pound's lines, their rambling yet probing tone – half-conversational, half-introspective – are like a flat demoralized echo of the impassioned disorder in some of Macbeth's or Cleopatra's speeches. The lines from Hopkins retain the passion – besides, of course, a serendipitous aptness for Shakespeare's tragic heroes.

In his essay 'The Music of Poetry', Eliot traced a double movement in Shakespeare's verse: from the artificiality of the earliest plays to the natural and colloquial, and thence to a new elaboration, versatile and humanly authentic. Eliot drew on this twofold resource not only in his plays but also in all his poetry. Sometimes Shakespeare appears at the surface, transformed by the context; sometimes he works below ground, like the ghost in *Hamlet*. The second section of *The Waste Land* taps many poetic veins, from the lushly mythic to the disquietingly realistic, all Shakespearean with varying overtness. It opens by adapting Enobarbus' account of Cleopatra on her barge (*Antony and Cleopatra*, 2.2.201–15) to describe a very different woman:

> The Chair she sat in, like a burnished throne,
> Glowed on the marble ...

The carving on the mantelpiece depicts

> The change of Philomel, by the barbarous king
> So rudely forced; ...
> And other withered stumps of time
> Were told upon the walls ...

The rape of Philomela suggests that of Lavinia in *Titus Andronicus*, even to the 'stumps' of the latter's chopped-off hands. Lavinia and Cleopatra mark the poles of Shakespeare's world of women, each a victim in her way. Eliot's lines encompass them both. Shakespeare reaches out to the poetic idiom of latter times, as though vindicating David Lodge's drunken researcher (in the 1984 novel *Small World*) into Eliot's influence upon Shakespeare. Here is Shakespeare's Lucrece after her rape:

> Her maid is gone, and she prepares to write,
> First hovering o'er the paper with her quill;
> Conceit and grief an eager combat fight,
> What wit sets down is blotted straight with will ...
>
> (*Lucrece*, 1296–9)

This simple, direct narration, with the woman's mental state woven into her distracted action, might belong to Eliot's time or indeed today. Here now is

Eliot's typist in *The Waste Land* after her unmemorable seduction by a house agent's clerk:

> She turns and looks a moment in the glass,
> Hardly aware of her departed lover;
> Her brain allows one half-formed thought to pass:
> 'Well now that's done: and I'm glad it's over.'

Did Eliot have Shakespeare's Lucrece in mind? We cannot tell, but a shared poetic register, underpinned by the parallel movement of the verse, makes the two women kin.

Later poets work the same two veins: direct allusions to Shakespeare, and more recondite echoes. Thom Gunn vividly depicts Shakespeare's age in 'A Mirror for Poets':

> It was a violent time. Wheels, racks, and fires
> In every writer's mouth.

Yet 'they found / Arcadia, a fruitful permanent land' of art, where 'mankind might behold its whole extent'.

> Here in a cave the Paphlagonian King
> Crouched, waiting for his greater counterpart
> Who one remove from likelihood may seem,
> But several nearer to the human heart.

The Paphlagonian King (from Philip Sidney's prose romance *Arcadia*) was the model for Gloucester in *King Lear*, reflecting as that character does Lear's own condition. Other poets turn Shakespeare's characters into symbols of their own time. Sidney Keyes, who died at twenty in World War II, presents Prospero with trenchant, understated bitterness: sensitive, philosophic, hence inured,

> far too wise to weep
> For fallen blossoms, or for youth that's gone.
>
> ('Prospero')

Geoffrey Hill evokes *Julius Caesar* no less cynically in his poem on a controversial French thinker, *The Mystery of the Charity of Charles Péguy*:

In Brutus' name martyr and mountebank
ghost Caesar's ghost, his wounds of air and ink
painlessly spouting.

Beyond such explicit allusion, we again enter the land of Shakespearean shadows. Could Philip Larkin have written 'Days' without thinking of Macbeth's 'To-morrow, and to-morrow, and to-morrow' (5.5.19–28)?

Days are where we live.
They come, they wake us
Time and time over. ...
Where can we live but days?

Ah, solving that question
Brings the priest and the doctor ...

Even an original like Dylan Thomas echoes Shakespeare's poem 'The Phoenix and Turtle' ('Let the bird of loudest lay / On the sole Arabian tree / Herald sad and trumpet be') in 'Unluckily for a death': 'unfired phoenix, herald / And heaven crier'. And in John Betjeman's 'Slough', the chillingly cheerful call 'Come, friendly bombs, and fall on Slough' urbanely revives memories of Timon's curses on corrupt Athens:

O thou wall
That girdles in those wolves, dive in the earth
And fence not Athens!
(*Timon of Athens*, 4.1.1–3; see also 4.1.1–41, 5.1.168–212)

It is even more challenging to assess Shakespeare's impact on languages other than his own. We can spot direct echoes and allusions. Any deeper absorption is hard to document, and a brief account must be drastically selective. I will cite only the most outstanding instance of Shakespeare's appeal across a culture, in Germany, focusing even there on a single figure, Heinrich Heine. I will then take up a more individual Shakespearean initiative by Yves Bonnefoy in France, and end with the remoter instance of Bengali poetry.

Germans claimed *unser Shakespeare* almost earlier than the English. Nine complete translations had appeared by 1839, besides a performance history starting in the seventeenth century. Reading the Bard, says Goethe's hero Wilhelm Meister in Book Three of *Wilhelm Meister's Apprenticeship*, is like standing before 'the unclosed awful Books of Fate, while the whirlwind of most impassioned life was howling through the leaves, and tossing them fiercely to and fro'. Wilhelm's analysis focuses on characterization and philosophy, but is impelled by the power of Shakespeare's poetry. This was effectively rendered by the poet, critic, and translator August Wilhelm Schlegel – ensuring, as a modern critic remarks, that Germans did not have to 'read [Shakespeare's] plays with the poetry left out'. Through Schlegel, Shakespeare left his imprint on the language of German poetry.

Yet Heine, the poet who imbibed Shakespeare most deeply, has only qualified praise for Schlegel. He forges his own engagement with Shakespeare, helped by acquaintance with the original and a stay in London where, like Keats, he was thrilled by Kean's performance. Special to Heine, making his Shakespearean legacy uncertain in specific passages but convincing in overall impact, is his tempering of romantic lyricism by a robustness grading into irony. Intense, even sentimental passion is shot through with betrayal and frustration in the short poem 'In den Küssen, welche Lüge':

> Though your protests overwhelm me,
> Still I know what you'll allow.
> Yet I'll swear by all you tell me;
> I'll believe all you avow.

Shakespeare's attachment to the Dark Lady was based on the same devoted suspension of mistrust, expressed in Sonnet 138: 'When my love swears that she is made of truth, / I do believe her, though I know she lies'. In a later poem ('Hat die Natur sich auch verschlechtert'), Heine, like Shakespeare in Sonnet 94, introduces lilies of tarnished purity, and the fawning dogs that occur through Shakespeare as an image of sycophancy.

Some borrowings are purely ironic, as when Gumpelino in Chapter Nine of Heine's (prose) *Baths of Lucca* swallows a laxative crying, like Romeo (5.3.119–20), 'O true apothecary, / Thy drugs are quick'. But there is a quizzical seriousness to the philosophic bear-hero Atta Troll's citing *Hamlet* (1.5.174–5):

More things lie 'twixt Earth and Heaven
Than philosophy may dream.

(Atta Troll, Canto 23)

In the Walpurgis-like 'wild hunt' in *Atta Troll*, the Bard himself is a rider, a winning smile on his face. In *Shakespeare's Maidens and Women* (1839), Heine extends the realm of Shakespearean drama, specifically the comedies, into a wider poetic universe where

> lords and ladies, shepherds and shepherdesses, fools and sages, wander about under the tall trees ... the lover and his loved one rest in the cool shadows and exchange tender words ... now and then a fabulous animal, perhaps a stag with silver horns, comes by ... And ... the water-ladies rise with green hair and glittering veils, and ... all at once the moon rises, and ... the nightingale trills.

This is a somewhat fanciful account of Shakespeare's world but a tolerably close one of Heine's own. The supernatural elements are prominent, for instance, in some poems set against the North Sea, or a ballad ('Wohl unter der Linde erklingt die Musik') of a merman and a 'nixie' dancing under the lindens with a merry company.

Cutting across periods, languages, genres (drama to lyric) and cultures (he had a strong distaste for the English), Heine finds congenial elements in Shakespeare from which to forge a compound all his own. This singular assimilation of one genius by another springs from the wider reception of Shakespeare in Germany. In our own day, the French poet Yves Bonnefoy has worked Shakespeare into a more personal poetic programme.

In an interview with John Naughton, Bonnefoy remarks how Shakespeare brilliantly performs the chief task of poetry: a 'war against conceptual representations', experiencing instead 'the immediacy of other beings', what Bonnefoy calls 'presence'. This is better embodied in the plays than the non-dramatic poems. Hence Bonnefoy renders the former in verse, the latter in prose. He finds the *Sonnets* restrictive in mode. By contrast, the passage where Mark Antony holds up Caesar's cloak to the populace and recalls when Caesar first wore it ("Twas on a summer's evening in his tent'; *Julius Caesar*, 3.2.170–95) conveys 'the lyrical essence of poetry'.

Of course there is a strong Shakespearean tradition in France, classically exemplified by Victor Hugo. But, says Bonnefoy in his essay 'Shakespeare and the French Poet', the French have only been 'told about' Shakespeare; they have not experienced 'the original tone of voice, that fusion of personal vision and word'. He takes up the challenge of rendering Shakespeare in French precisely because of the 'opposing metaphysics' of the two languages. What then, in his own poetry, can he authentically derive from Shakespeare?

There are figures and motifs from *A Midsummer Night's Dream* in *Pierre écrite* (1965), from *The Winter's Tale* in *Dans le leurre du seuil* (1975), and from *Hamlet* in *L'heure présente* (2011). Beyond that, one can only chase ghosts. What might Helen in 'De vent et de fumée' (*La Vie errante*, 1993) owe to *Troilus and Cressida*? In 'Justice', is the 'beautiful country' where all roads end akin to Hamlet's 'undiscover'd country, from whose bourn / No traveller returns' (3.1.79–80)? Was 'the sound of a lamp, / By the bright threshold of an isolated house' in 'Vrai lieu' suggested by the candle throwing its beams in *The Merchant of Venice* (5.1.90), in a context full of the sound of music? In 'Douve parle', is it Lear's voice saying 'Let the coldness by my death arise and take on a meaning', recalling the heath with its 'aridness blown across / Only by the wind of the finite'? Bonnefoy repeatedly uses *finitude* for our feeble, limited, contingent mortality, which yet conveys the full and unmediated 'presence' of the human condition. Where does this appear better than in *King Lear*?

If tracking Shakespeare's footsteps in French poetry is a tentative exercise, how much more so in a more distant language and culture. India has the longest Shakespearean tradition of any non-Western country, impacting on poetry and drama in the country's many tongues. In Bengali, the language of Rabindranath Tagore, Shakespeare's example brought a new infusion of poetry to a traditional drama not unlike the Elizabethan: the texture of its verse dialogue was refashioned and enriched for a new urban, Western-style theatre. Tagore's early plays follow this model (his tutor made him translate *Macbeth* as a boy), but he moved on to a totally new vein of symbolic drama. In fact, he was not especially devoted to Shakespeare. His sonnet to the Bard (translated for *A Book of Homage to Shakespeare*, 1916) is fulsome but, by that very token, somewhat formal. His best-known critique of Shakespeare is an essay, 'Shakuntala', comparing Miranda unfavourably with Kalidasa's

Shakuntala in spiritual and ethical terms. There are many references to Shakespeare in his vast corpus, but hardly one clear poetic echo.

Like the late Shakespeare, the late Tagore explores a directness of speech and a silence beyond all speech:

> The stage lights fade one by one, the theatre empties.
> The finger of silence signals my soul to a quietude
> Like the slumber of dreamscapes blotted out by the ink of darkness.
>
> (*Prantik*, poem 8; my translation)

This reminds us of Prospero's epilogue in *The Tempest* ('Now my charms are all o'erthrown'), and still more his speech about an 'insubstantial pageant' dissolving like 'the great globe' that is at once the world and Shakespeare's playhouse (4.1.148–58). In Tagore's poem, such dissolution marks a fulfilment rather than an erasure:

> When the earth's painted lines are lost in the emptiness of day's end,
> The emancipated sky is still with wordless wonder
> At the starlit recognition of its own self.

Shakespeare and Tagore both express a profound sense of closure through comparable settings of word and image, a shared *poetic* vein beneath divergent concepts and contexts; but they reach this point by utterly different paths.

It is Tagore's Modernist successors who explicitly return to Shakespeare. Like the English Modernists, they prize Shakespeare's knots and ironies. Moreover, writing in another language, they can use his linguistic otherness to generate a complexity absent in the original. Like all appropriators, they use him to explore the poetic resources of their own language. Sudhindranath Datta, famous for his abstruse diction, does this *in extenso* in translations of 23 sonnets. In Bishnu Dey's 'Cressida', Troilus's love-lament becomes a dirge for a shattered, conflict-riven world, with clear strains from Shakespeare's play:

> My heart is a rider on the next world's ferry.
> Helmsman-less, my eyes burn from the far shore's sand.
>
> (My translation)

(Shakespeare: 'I stalk about her door / Like a strange soul upon the Stygian banks / Staying for waftage. O, be thou my Charon'; *Troilus and Cressida* 3.2.7–9); or

> Time's bag has a hundred holes, bored by oblivion's worm.

(Shakespeare: 'Time hath, my lord, a wallet at his back, / Wherein he puts alms for oblivion'; 3.3.147–8); or, evoking the scenes (4.5.14–64; 5.2.7–112) of Cressida among the Greeks,

> Not even in bad dreams had hope feared this:
> Naked speech in the virgin's downcast eyes,
> Her face, her body, in the enemy camp!
> O Greek lover, today you have vanquished Troy.

Such poems mark the dispersal of Shakespeare's poetry in a land far from its first home.

Shakti Chattopadhyay's sonnet (see my translation, reproduced below) is a notable cultural marker for many reasons. Shakti sees Rome as part of the East: Shakespeare does not care if the 'Eastern' Cinna is torn by the mob in *Julius Caesar*. Again, reversing the usual valuation, 'poetry's trade' is seen as a more worldly, workaday activity than 'theatre's art': hence too the poet Cinna deserves no mercy. But Shakespeare cannot get off so lightly: he must expose the 'black soul' of his own country in the history plays (actually written before *Julius Caesar*).

The last reason is pivotal: the very fact that a poet from Bengal in 1970 can address Shakespeare familiarly as 'William', and have his own take on a Roman play by this English dramatist written some 370 years earlier. Shakti's abrasive irony contrasts with the somewhat florid eulogy of Tagore's sonnet to Shakespeare from an earlier generation. Even the juggling with geography and chronology has a positive function: it is a specially striking instance of how Shakespeare can be translocated in time and space. This is amply recognized in world theatre, but that is a relatively well-defined sphere. It is even more telling that Shakespeare should be so variously naturalized in the total universe of the world's poetry.

Leaving aside direct allusion to the plays, this is at one level a matter of language: the adoption of phrases, images and verbal registers. But only so much and no more of verbal practice can be imported from one language into another. More basically, the enduring presence of Shakespeare's poetry is owing to its core imaginative quality: a power to comprehend nature and human life that validates itself in many ages and cultures. Hence it can be endlessly restated in the languages of those ages and cultures. That is why Shakespeare's poetry has endless afterlives.

Sonnet 86

Shakti Chattopadhyay

You are responsible for Cinna's death –
You, William: why expose the poet to angry Rome,
Among the streets infested with the hounds
Of treason, loot, murder? William, you sprang from the same loam!

Your heart is torn between the theatre's art
And poetry's trade: so did the poem-enraptured Cinna
Die in the tussle? O West, do you seek in the East
Of drama and counter-drama the twilight-zone dilemma?

Or did the Avon banks for England beg,
And you, good masochist, kill yourself to that end –
Leaving self-scribblings, showing instead the black soul
Of the state? You'll go far this way too, my friend.

You are Greece, you are William – epic poet unfollowed.
In drama-bereft Bengal may your name be hallowed.

Translated from the Bengali by Sukanta Chaudhuri

3

Shakespeare and Music

Tom Bishop

A full account of the 'creative legacy' of Shakespeare in Western music might require something like a history of that music itself, since there is hardly a corner of musical production since Shakespeare's death that has not been touched in some way or other by responsiveness to his work. The five-volume *Shakespeare Music Catalogue* of Bryan Gooch and David Thatcher lists over 20,000 items, while the invaluable online resource The LiederNet Archive (http://www.lieder.net/, curated by Emily Ezust), which catalogues settings of lyrics from the Western art-music tradition, lists versions of the short poem 'Take, o take those lips away' from *Measure for Measure* (4.1.1–6) by some eighty-three different composers, stretching back to the earliest surviving setting by John Wilson (1652) – though there must have been still earlier ones, since the song appears in the play. Of those eighty-three composers, several set the poem more than once, and the roster includes settings not only in English, but also in German (in four different translations), French (in three), Dutch (in two), Finnish and Polish. This may be an unusually rich instance, but it suggests the sheer weight of material translated from Shakespeare into music.

The task is hard in another way also. A proper anatomy would require not merely a large catalogue of instances, but an account of the wide variety of modes – itself a musical metaphor – by which one artist's work may respond to another's. A simple vocabulary will hardly suffice, particularly where the relation, as in this case, is not merely across time but also across media. We would need to be able to specify with some precision what differences we meant to indicate in the relations between a Shakespearean and a musical work by such terms as influence, citation, borrowing, echo, recollection, allusion, adaptation, appropriation, and so on. Elgar calling a large-scale symphonic study *Falstaff* (1913) is one thing, and the manner of its evocation of Shakespeare's fat knight is part of a fairly public conversation. But there are subtler links that may be just as important for all their elusiveness. When Carl Amenda reports that his friend Beethoven composed the slow movement of his early String Quartet (Op. 18, No. 1; 1801) in response to the burial-vault scene of *Romeo and Juliet* – a claim supported by a manuscript sketch-leaf on which the composer wrote 'les derniers soupirs' ('the last sighs') over an especially poignant descending passage – the creative conversation at work is much more slippery and inward, much more difficult to describe. And suppose we did not have those witnesses? The elaboration of Beethoven's tragic idiom in relation to Shakespeare's example would then have been none the less real, but hidden from us by an accident of history.

It is clear that Shakespeare was particularly alive to the expressive resources of the music of his day – more so, indeed, than any of his fellow playwrights. Ross Duffin's *Shakespeare's Songbook* has shown how saturated by contemporary song his works are. Characters at all levels have access to songs of one kind or another, from popular ballad to sophisticated 'art song', as we might now say, and they are used for purposes across a full range of complexity. Not only does he incorporate music for song, for dancing, and for 'spiritual' or 'atmospheric' effects in his plays – such as the revival of Hermione in *The Winter's Tale* – but he also explores the availability of music itself to open up different registers of figuration from those of speech or movement. The central point about music for Shakespeare would seem to have been his response to polyphony – not so much in the technical sense of independent voices in counterpoint, but in the provision of several different layers or strands of expressivity at once, interacting with one another to uniquely complex effect. This complexity was strikingly like his own mature conception both of linguistic semantics and of psychology, though it would be impossible to demonstrate to what extent music was a key factor in this development. For Shakespeare, then, a profoundly dialectical thinker, music was a uniquely expressive case of the central insight that there is never only one object, one resonance, one meaning. Each moment, word, person comprises a dynamic set of leadings and potential realizations. Macbeth is at once a traitor and a loyal subject, Rosalind at once a lover and a spurner of love, Richard III at once a monster and a clown. His lyrics ring multiple changes on what he elsewhere calls 'Single nature's double name' ('The Phoenix and Turtle', 39). His plays develop polyphonic effects in which elements are placed in complicated relations of similarity and difference. Sometimes they are very explicit about the musical analogy available for this aspect of their design. Duke Theseus, in *A Midsummer Night's Dream*, arranges a concert of hunting dogs for his fiancée, Hippolyta, and invites her to take pleasure in 'the musical confusion / Of hounds and echo in conjunction' (4.1.109–10) at just the point in the play when the confusions of its own plot have attained a maximum; and later, confronted with the apparent cacophony of '*very tragical mirth*', he asks 'How shall we find the concord of this discord?' (5.1.57, 60) – a question that bears as much on the play as on the immediate occasion.

For Shakespeare's depiction of character as a uniquely complex knot of impulses, plumbed and unplumbed, music also provided an area of analogy. This is especially so for those characters – like fools, and women in tragedy – for whom the resources of direct speech are less available. Lear's Fool finds there are insights he can better deliver to his beloved master in song than in speech. And when Desdemona and Ophelia turn, and turn *from*, their suffering into song, their music not only sweetens their state, as those around them tend to perceive it, but also immeasurably sharpens what they have to say, in ways that they themselves may only half intend, and that the decorums of the play can only allow through a musical displacement. Musical representation puts on display, for them and for Shakespeare, what must be said and not said at once. At such moments, the complexity of musical utterance comes close to disclosing the complexly polyphonic character of experience itself.

If the expressive resources of music were an integral part of Shakespeare's creative awareness, it is hardly surprising that composers were, even in his lifetime, already responding to the potential of his work for musical elaboration. Though Thomas Morley's setting of 'It was a lover and his lass' (publ. 1597) may possibly be independent of *As You like It*, where the same song-text appears at 5.3.15, Robert Johnson's settings of later lyrics, such as his famous versions of Ariel's songs in *The Tempest*, are clearly tied to the plays, and were probably performed in them. A continuous and ever-widening array of song settings can be traced from Johnson to the present day, both for use in play performance and not. And more general musical supplementation of the plays seems also to have begun very early, possibly even with the playwright's consent, and certainly by 1623 when the Folio publication of *Macbeth* (the only text we have) shows the play had already absorbed two song-and-dance numbers from Middleton's *The Witch* (unpubl. 1609–16?) to amplify its popular witchcraft scenes. We have little information on what other musical supplements and alterations might have followed before the theatres were closed in 1642, but it seems at least likely that dances and other music would have been varied for periodic revivals, in line with developing fashions. Wilson's setting of 'Take, o take' may suggest as much.

Certainly, the proliferation of musical enhancements to Shakespeare's plays is marked in the changed theatrical culture after the 1660 restoration of the monarchy, which saw musical additions and migrations affecting both familiar plays and others less so. As operatic responses to Shakespeare are treated elsewhere in this volume, they will not feature here, but it is worth noting that for quite some time the relations among opera, play with music, masque, dance suite and so on remained fluid. *The Tempest,* in Shadwell's version (1674) of Dryden and Davenant's staging, became essentially what we might now call a 'musical', and *A Midsummer Night's Dream* was transformed into *The Fairy Queen* (1692), a version of the play with musical scenes by Purcell 'interluded' into it. *Macbeth*, in Davenant's revised version (1664), acquired much additional music along with spectacular flying witches. Nor, in all probability, do we have a full picture. Jeremiah Clarke's music for, of all things, *Titus Andronicus* (1696?) only survives as two pieces, but was probably once fuller. And the influence of Shakespearean example on music production may also be indirect. John Blow's *Venus and Adonis* (1683), variously described as a masque, a semi-opera and the first surviving English opera, may owe something to the example of Shakespeare's poem on the same subject, while Nahum Tate's libretto for Purcell's *Dido and Aeneas* (1688?) certainly nods towards *Macbeth* in introducing two scenes for witches that make nonsense of Virgil's original parable of national destiny. That Purcell's work was thought suitable for interluding within Charles Gildon's 1700 version of *Measure for*

Measure (sub-titled *Beauty the Best Advocate*) may also suggest that some Shakespearean connection was recognized.

This fluidity of relations between Shakespeare's plays and musical composition continues well into the eighteenth century. Even those plays that – unlike *The Tempest* and *A Midsummer Night's Dream* in various adapted versions – were not effectively transformed into quasi-musical works were surrounded by, and in many cases filled out with, musical material in songs, dances and so on. Musical afterpieces of various kinds, from masques to comic pantomime, became standard fare in theatrical entertainment, like the comic jigs that had once concluded performances at Elizabethan playhouses. Amid this jostling, numerous dance settings, instrumental suites, and song-texts for or related to Shakespeare's plays sustain a more or less continuous production through the late seventeenth and the eighteenth century, and also progressively become detached from theatrical performance to be published by themselves. Much, though not all, of the music by Thomas Arne originally written for the stage was later published, and several pieces, especially songs, are still well known. Arne's work covers a wide range of the adapted repertory, and was supplemented by his choruses and recitative accompaniment for Garrick's Jubilee recitation of his 'Ode upon Dedicating a Building and Erecting a Statue, to Shakespeare, at Stratford Upon Avon' (1769), fixing the composer's claim on an official Shakespearean mantle. With the gradual installation of Shakespeare as a national poet during the latter part of the century, such 'para-Shakespearean' compositions are found more frequently, such as the 'Lyric Ode on the Fairies, Aerial Beings and Witches of Shakespeare' (1776) for soloists, chorus, and orchestra by the ill-fated nineteen-year-old Thomas Linley Jr. ('the English Mozart'), following up his equally remarkable music for Garrick's revival of *The Tempest* from two years earlier. There is hardly an English composer of this period who does not have one Shakespeare-related piece to his credit. The striking absence from the roster is Handel, who never set a text from or for a Shakespearean work, for unknown reasons, though he did set other English poets, such as Milton. Works that celebrate rather than just illustrate Shakespeare are not, of course, confined to the eighteenth century, but continue to be composed, especially around large public celebrations: Elgar composed 'Shakespeare's Kingdom' for the 1924 British

Empire Exhibition, and Peter Maxwell Davies his 'Shakespeare Music' for the 1964 centenary.

A good sense of how English musical culture framed Shakespeare's creative legacy at the end of the eighteenth century – just at the start of its remarkable efflorescence on the Continent – can be deduced from Haydn's response, guided by his friend and lyricist Anne Hunter. During Haydn's time in London he came in contact with the English vogue of 'canzonetta' songs to piano accompaniment. He contributed two sets of six songs (1794 and 1795), plus two additional single items when he returned to Austria (1801 and 1803). The song texts were overwhelmingly Mrs. Hunter's, in established styles of English lyric (sea song, pastoral, lament, gothic, etc.). The fourth of the second set, however, fitting itself to these tastes, was Viola's speech – 'she never told her love' – from *Twelfth Night* (2.5.111), which Haydn set plangently as an elegy, with expressive weight in the piano part unfolding his exploration of the heroine's secret feelings. Further, Haydn apparently believed that the text for 'The Spirit's Song', the 1801 work published first in German, was also by Shakespeare. The mistake suggests that Haydn's sense of 'the Shakespearean' lay especially in tragic pathos and the supernatural.

Haydn's songs effectively prefigure, if indeed they did not directly influence, later Continental settings of Shakespearean lyric, such as Schubert's 'An Sylvia'. By that time, however, the flood of Shakespearean fictions into Continental literatures – what Jane Moody calls his 'transcontinental migration' – was well advanced. It may conveniently be represented by the various appearances of Oberon and Titania from Shakespeare in Wieland's 1780 romance *Oberon*; in the Danish opera *Holger Danske* (1789) and the Walpurgisnacht scene of Goethe's *Faust Part One* (1808); and, finally, in Weber's opera *Oberon* (1826), which, returning home, was written in England for Covent Garden, to an English libretto by the costume designer James Planché and which was nominally based on Wieland but included Puck!

Haydn's songs also point the way to the inexhaustible stream of song settings that now extends to composers from all parts of the world and for a wide variety of solo, accompanied solo and variously combined ensembles, in many languages, idioms and textures. Anglophone music has, not surprisingly, been especially rich in these, both in Britain and worldwide, and the roster reads like a roll call of composers: Sullivan, Parry, Stanford, Vaughan Williams, Quilter, Ireland, Howells, Tippett, Britten, Heseltine (aka 'Warlock'), Birtwistle, Benjamin and, from outside the UK, David Amram (USA), Arlene Zallman (USA), Richard Faith (USA), David Hamilton (NZ), Peter Sculthorpe (Australia), Hendryk Hofmeyr (South Africa), and Allan Bevan (Canada). As if to prove the rule, prominent names missing above – Elgar, Holst, Delius, Maxwell Davies, Adès, for instance – often turn out to have worked with Shakespearean material in larger formats. Similarly impressive lists of songs by non-Anglophone composers could also be constructed, from Schumann and Brahms, to Stravinsky and Shostakovich, to de Leeuw and Mäntyjärvi. Such lists testify at once to the wealth and adaptability of Shakespeare for musical purposes and the centrality of his work as a resource and an orientation point for composers, though no doubt the impressive list of predecessors who have already worked this field establishes a certain momentum and attractive gravity.

We can return to the 1826 Weber *Oberon* premiere, with its odd, sidelong relation to Shakespeare, as a switch-point in tracing the impact of Shakespeare on Western music along another and slightly different line of development from the song setting: those related genres, departing more or less from the same year, that comprise the concert overture, the symphonic poem, the orchestral suite, the fantasia and so on. With important prefigurations, including the *Oberon* overture itself, we may also locate Shakespeare's creative legacy as a primary impetus to this development, separate from that of the symphony proper, in which Shakespeare hardly figures.

Mendelssohn's overture to *A Midsummer Night's Dream* was perhaps prompted by Weber's from earlier the same year – the two composers were close friends, despite a large gap in age. The piece is justly famous, though it was worked almost to death in productions over many years. It was used in Max Reinhardt's film of the play in 1935, and remains a concert repertory and choreography staple. Its key importance as an early and thoroughly successful version of the freestanding concert overture makes all the more notable that it took Shakespeare's play for its subject. There are few earlier examples, though we should note that Beethoven's *Coriolan* overture (1807), written for a revival of a mediocre and soon-forgotten play by Collin, was assimilated to the inspiration of Shakespeare's tragedy by both Berlioz and Wagner – and, conceivably, by Beethoven himself. Once more we encounter the twin poles of tragic pathos and supernatural brio.

But the key event for the future unfolding of a Shakespearean legacy in this area of composition was surely the thunderous impact, by his own report, of Shakespeare on Hector Berlioz in 1827, with the Paris performances by William Abbot's company, and, above all, by Harriet Smithson, its leading lady, whom Berlioz later married. The importance of this occasion for Berlioz is well known and could hardly be exaggerated. From our perspective, it allows us to watch Berlioz taking a quite different line from his predecessors in responding to this key artistic influence, not only in the Shakespeare-related works the epiphany generated from him but in his wider sense of musical form and aesthetic purpose. For Berlioz, that is, Shakespeare was not only a major established occasion for the exercise of compositional prowess in certain areas of feeling and subject, he became also, through the intimate knowledge and reflection of the composer on the plays (and Berlioz became an acknowledged French authority), a source of compositional ideas, and even strategies. In the heady atmosphere of French Romanticism's systematic attack on inherited systems of decorum and genre, Berlioz was the first musician to consider the implications of Shakespeare's work both for the design of an individual composition and for issues of musical aesthetics in general. It is clear from various remarks that throughout his life he responded vigorously to what he saw as the musical implications of Shakespeare's work – as with his remark of 1859 describing Juliet's speech before taking the sleeping potion as 'Shakespeare's stupendous crescendo – he was indeed the inventor of the crescendo'. In another composer one might take this as an offhand analogy; in Berlioz's case it looks more like the expression of an aesthetic affinity. Several aspects of his compositional style might well be taken as intimately involved with his intense engagement with Shakespeare. For instance, what Robert Lawrence called his 'amazing use simultaneously not so much of several contrapuntal lines as of diverse planes of musical experience' suggests the Shakespearean strategy of juxtaposing within the same action strongly diverse perspectives in close relation.

Berlioz's catalogue eventually included responses to *Hamlet*, *The Tempest*, *Romeo and Juliet*, *King Lear*, *The Merchant of Venice* (disguised as a love-scene in *The Trojans*) and *Much Ado About Nothing*. He also contemplated operas based on *Hamlet*, *Othello* and *Antony and Cleopatra* (and his 1829 cantata *La Mort de Cléopatre*, though to a text of Vieillard, carries a Shakespearean epigraph). But his energetic relation to Shakespeare was active even outside nominally Shakespearean compositions. Thus, though the *Symphonie fantastique* of 1830 is not directly shaped from Shakespearean material or exemplar – being more akin in its programme to Goethe's *Faust*, which also strongly affected Berlioz – it has strongly Shakespearean associations. It was written in the intoxicating days of Berlioz's encounter with Shakespeare and of his romantic passion for Smithson, and it features vividly those aspects of his compositional style that Berlioz himself singled out as particularly his, and presumably admired in Shakespeare, namely 'passionate expression, inward intensity, rhythmic impetus, and a quality of unexpectedness'.

Less speculatively, one can speak of the decisive influence of Berlioz's programme of non-symphonic orchestral music, oriented in particular around Shakespeare in his series of concert pieces, on the development of the symphonic poem in later decades. *Lélio; or the Return to Life* (1832), his sequel to the *Symphonie fantastique*, warmly received but now little performed, weaves several pieces of Shakespeare-inflected material through its unprecedented six-part structure of theatrical, spoken, sung and played sections, imagining a kind of antidote or counter-magic to the baleful hysteria of the *Symphonie* by infusing it with Shakespearean analogues. The work's composer-narrator, in some sort an image of Berlioz-as-Prospero, frequently refers to Shakespeare, in particular to *Hamlet* and *The Tempest*, and an extended orchestral fantasy on the latter play concludes the work, recapitulating and glossing its larger movement from exile to reintegration. Peter Bloom rightly calls it Berlioz's 'most Shakespearean work'.

More influential, perhaps because somewhat less radical in form, was the 'dramatic symphony', *Roméo et Juliette* (1839), which was both an immediate and lasting success. Richard Wagner was in its first audience in Paris and never forgot it, having already himself written an unsuccessful opera based on *Measure for Measure* (*Das Liebesverbot*, 1834). Indeed, one emblem of Berlioz's transmission of a Shakespearean 'creative legacy' may be traced in the startlingly close recollection of the opening melody of Part Two of this work ('Roméo seul') in the famous opening motif of Wagner's *Tristan und Isolde* (1857–9; perf. 1865). Like Berlioz, Wagner identified his own creative work closely with Shakespeare, whom he called 'my only kindred spirit' ('meine einziger Geistes-Freund'). The *Tristan* motif itself reappears, metrically modulated and textured in a way once more reminiscent of Berlioz, in the famous 'Adagio' of Khachaturian's *Gayane* ballet (1942), which may therefore be a sort of distant descendant of Romeo's solitude.

The importance of these works by Berlioz for later development of the 'symphonic poem' genre would be hard to overstate. Liszt, who met Berlioz the day before the *Symphonie* was first played, and who persuaded him to revise and publish *Lélio* in 1855, just as he himself was developing the 'symphonic poem', added his own Shakespearean exemplar in his *Hamlet* of 1858, prompting a succession of related works by Smetana (*Richard III*, 1858), Richard Strauss (*Macbeth*, 1888), Dvorak (*Othello*, 1892), and Elgar (*Falstaff*, 1913). Berlioz's significance for the dissemination of Shakespeare in orchestral music may also be associated with its efflorescence in Russia, which Berlioz twice visited, meeting composers and conducting his music. Here, too, Shakespeare features prominently, with Balakirev's *King Lear* (1859) and, more famously, Tchaikovsky's *Romeo and Juliet* (1870–80), *The Tempest* (1873), and *Hamlet* (1888; to which he added further music in 1891).

Like song-settings, then, large-scale orchestral pieces taking Shakespeare's works as subject have become a regular part of the repertoire. After Berlioz, such orchestral compositions used the scope and texture of his work much more comprehensively, in a tradition of writing that has continued and diversified. Hans Werner Henze's three-movement *Eighth Symphony* (1983) is modelled from *A Midsummer Night's Dream*. The Australian composer Gordon Kerry has recently produced three deft and elegant orchestral symphonic poems – *Such sweet thunder* (1999), *This insubstantial pageant* (2003), and *In restless ecstasy* (2006) – in response to a familiar trio of *A Midsummer Night's Dream*, *The Tempest*, and *Macbeth*. Works for smaller forces also, even those as reduced as Henze's *Royal Winter Music* (1976 and 1979), a pair of multi-movement 'sonatas' for solo guitar presenting short character pieces on Shakespearean characters, might also be regarded as developments of this tradition.

Related to this line of instrumental pieces (by whatever name these are known – overture, tone poem, suite, fantasia, etc.) are the various 'incidental musics' for productions, real or imagined, that also overlap with musical treatments of the plays intended for ballet companies and with scores produced for films. Attempting to make categorical distinctions among these is unhelpful, since achievements in one area are often taken up and reworked in another. Theatre, ballet and, more recently, film scores often reappear in concert in the form of orchestral compilations, suites or adaptations, or are simply played or released as excerpts, as with Toru Takemitsu's remarkable score for Kurosawa's *Ran* (1985), a version of *King Lear*. Music for one play may even be adapted for another, and these interactions can get quite complicated. Thus Shostakovich's music for Akimov's 1931 production of *Hamlet* was reworked as a small suite for orchestra, while his music for Kosintsev's *King Lear* production in the besieged Leningrad of 1941 was recycled in the same director's 1954 staging of *Hamlet*, and the composer, of course, later produced new music for the director's films of *Hamlet* (1964; but this music was first heard in a concert in Gorky) and *King Lear* (1971). 'Incidental music' – a term that became current in the nineteenth century – is now generally used for an organized suite of pieces evoking a play, thematically linked, and marked with the authority of a single composer. Such groupings may or may not be associated with an actual staging. Beethoven's *Egmont* music – the clearest precursor of the genre – was for a production, as were Mendelssohn's *A Midsummer Night's Dream* music, written sixteen years after the 1826 overture, and Korngold's *Much Ado* suite (1918–19; also arranged for violin and piano). But Arthur Sullivan's music for *The Tempest* (1861) was his graduation piece from the Leipzig Conservatory, and Sibelius's late masterpiece, *The Tempest* (1926), though nominally 'incidental music' and conceived for a proposed production, is hardly suited for a performance of the play at over an hour long. Alexei Ratmansky, however, did choreograph a ballet to it in 2013.

Contemporary play productions continue to commission, invent and deploy their own music, in addition to using borrowed material via modern recording technologies. They can also do without music entirely. Not so danced versions of Shakespeare. Dance music for use within the plays dates from very early, and Shakespeare ballets stretch back at least as far as Lepicq's *Macbeth* in London and Luzzi's *Romeo and Juliet* in Venice (both 1785). But the international development of dance as a premier stand-alone performance art led to the wide adoption of Shakespeare's plays as subjects, especially in the twentieth century, attracting new music as well as reusing earlier scores. Robert Helpman's innovative *Hamlet* (Sadler's Wells, 1942) used Tchaikovsky's overture, and *A Midsummer Night's Dream* ballets using Mendelssohn have been devised by Petipa (Imperial Ballet, St. Petersburg, 1876), Ashton (Royal Ballet, 1964), Balanchine (New York City Ballet, 1962), and, most recently, by Liam Scarlett (Royal New Zealand Ballet, 2015). Florent Schmitt, on the other hand, wrote new dance music for André Gide's 1920 Paris Opera adaptation of *Antony and Cleopatra*, from which he derived two suites, and Prokofiev adapted three suites from his ballet music for *Romeo and Juliet*, which has also been re-choreographed over ten times since its 1940 premiere (e.g. Ashton for Danish Royal Ballet, 1955; Cranko for the Stuttgart Ballet, 1962; Macmillan for the Royal Ballet, 1965; Grigorovitch for the Bolshoi, 1979; Martins for the New York City Ballet, 2007). There may indeed be something of a high moment in Shakespeare-based ballets at present. Recent works include Crystal Pite's *The Tempest Replica* (2011; score by Owen Belton), Christopher Wheeldon's *The Winter's Tale* (Royal Ballet, 2014, score by Joby Talbot) and Jean-Christoph Maillot, *The Taming of the Shrew* (Bolshoi, 2014, score arranged from Shostakovich's 1958 operetta *Cheryomushki*). Among the most innovative of these recent works is Doug Elkins's *Mo(or)town/Redux* (2011), a dance version of *Othello* set to a score of Motown music, and itself responding to José Limon's *Othello* ballet, *The Moor's Pavane* (1949), which used music of Purcell written for a 1695 revival of Behn's *Abdelazar; or The Moor's Revenge* (1676), an adaptation of the old anonymous play *Lust's Dominion* (of about 1600)!

The example of Elkins's work with *Othello*, and its complicated prehistory, brings us to the interaction between Shakespearean fictions and popular music. As with the other musical genres, Shakespeare has provided rich opportunities here, taken up in a wide variety of ways, that often blur or cross boundaries. Again there is a bewildering array of examples that seem to comprise an extended and multiform conversation among both artists and expressive possibilities rather than anything that can be simply or coherently summarized. Shakespeare provides a set of common stories and figures, mostly centred on a smaller number of the more familiar plays, that are passed back and forth repeatedly among artists and genres. Experiments and explorations, some highly productive and some flatly disastrous, are plentiful, and it may be that Shakespearean fictions are now so familiar and established that they have become topoi or commonplaces, trailing certain kinds of cultural authority, to be sure, but also generally available, and robust enough to accommodate almost any artistic intention. For the 1938 film *The Goldwyn Follies*, George Gershwin wrote music for a version of *Romeo and Juliet* in which the Capulets and Montagues are rival hotel owners who advocate classical ballet and tap-dancing, respectively, and the sequence ends with an upbeat danced reconciliation between the families. *Catch My Soul*, a rock-and-roll musical of *Othello* staged in the US in 1968 and the UK in 1969, originally starred William Marshall as Othello and Jerry Lee Lewis as Iago. In 1973 it was released as an unsuccessful film, set in New Mexico and with Richie Havens as Othello. But Cole Porter's music for *Kiss Me Kate* (1949; movie 1953) and Bernstein's for *West Side Story* (1957; movie 1961) are widely popular and familiar versions of *The Taming of the Shrew* and *Romeo and Juliet*. Duke Ellington and Billy Strayhorn's album, *Such Sweet Thunder* (1957), is one of the central works of jazz history. Structured as twelve numbers each depicting a different Shakespearean character, it could be said to be a series of compressed jazz tone-poems. In 1960 it was staged as a ballet for TV by Maurice Béjart. Elvis Costello released his own music for a ballet version of *A Midsummer Night's Dream (Il Sogno)* in 1980. A punk/indie band, formed in 2005 in Glen Rock, New Jersey, calls itself 'Titus Andronicus'. And so on.

Such lists could be protracted almost indefinitely: Shakespeare continues to be not only musical in himself, but a cause why music is in others. A final emblem of the productive relation of Shakespeare to popular music may be seen in Mark Knopfler's well-known song, 'Romeo and Juliet' (Dire Straits, *Making Movies*, 1980), so often covered by other musicians. The song is not at all a straightforward version of Shakespeare's tragedy, but instead an ironic embedding of the old story within another, more modern one, to figure and measure the embittered passion of a failed love much closer, in the end, to that of Troilus and Cressida. In the new song several other versions of popular romance are echoed, including Bernstein's own response to the same founding tale. The song is canny about this allusive procedure, even quoting its Juliet in casual summary of the new anti-romance as 'Oh, Romeo, yeah, you know / I used to have a scene with him'. In the rich use to which the new song puts the old tale, we may trace the particular flexibility and openness to successors that Shakespeare's work still fosters as its legacy to music.

4

Shakespeare and Dance

David Fuller

Shakespeare without words. Shakespeare in dance involves that paradox: Shakespeare without that by which he is most himself – poetry. It might seem more problematic even than *Hamlet* without the Prince. But, without words, might we see more of what a Shakespeare play thought of as a *text* – Shakespeare as he rarely saw his work, as a book – may obscure: the play as narrative structure, embodied movement, sequence of tones and tableaux, and emblematic stage picture. Released from conventions of naturalistic acting style that dominate in contemporary theatre, might we apprehend the symbolic or epitomic aspects of Shakespeare's stagecraft, which are still operative in the more evidently stylized medium of dance as, in contemporary verbal theatre, they rarely are. As Nietzsche writes of *Hamlet*: 'the structure of the scenes and the vivid images reveal a deeper wisdom than the poet ... can put into words and concepts' (*The Birth of Tragedy*, §17). Romeo and Juliet, Hamlet, and other Shakespearean characters clearly function as cultural myths for people who have never read Shakespeare's words. Important as words are, the meaning of any play as a whole lies not only in words but also in the structured sequence of embodied actions and images, gestures and tableaux, and all the ways in which these interact with and comment on the words. Shakespeare ballets are first of all creative outgrowths of the works on which they are based, meaningful in their own terms. They may also be forms of investigative critical response, ways of thinking about meaning in poetic drama.

For this, those to whom dance-theatre is unfamiliar may need to peer somewhat into an aesthetic darkness – but that is many people's situation much of the time, and it is a situation that can be valuable, free of rehearsed response. Looking through learned techniques is not always the best way to see freshly: a living machine to think with is kept in a state of supple operation by the challenge of the New. And, even more than in the fluidity of verbal theatre, in dance meaning is unfixed, offers opportunities for – even makes inevitable – variety of signification and response. The ways in which a ballet prompts ideas about the play on which it is based may be straightforward: dance reveals some aspect of the drama with special vividness. Even adaptations based purely on the internal dynamics of dance can prompt fresh understandings – as with ballets that attempt to evoke the fundamental emotions of their source without its specific narrative triggers.

Ballet is a form in which Shakespeare has had rich creative impact partly because some of the plays have inherent potential for dance – in fundamental emotions that are powerfully communicable by movement; in their modulation, juxtaposition and contrasts of tone; in their narrative and dramatic structures. Early adaptations of Shakespeare often incorporated extended opportunities for dance (Dryden's and Davenant's *The Tempest*; Purcell's *The Fairy Queen* [*A Midsummer Night's Dream*]). With the exception of the English and Roman Histories, a full range of Shakespeare's work has been danced, sometimes in several versions (*The Taming of the Shrew, Hamlet, Othello*), and recently with new interest in works not previously much presented in dance, from the *Sonnets* to *The Tempest*. *A Midsummer Night's Dream*, perhaps because of its broad contrasts of mode and tone (supernatural, mortal-romantic, mortal-comic) and *Romeo and Juliet*, perhaps because of its subjects (violent conflict, the romantic-erotic), have been especially amenable to being recreated in dance – though a significant influence in their popularity with choreographers has also been the wonderfully danceable scores of Mendelssohn and Prokofiev.

A Midsummer Night's Dream

Probably the most often performed choreography of *A Midsummer Night's Dream* is by George Balanchine (1962). Best known for abstract dance,

Balanchine was not always good at narrative, and the second of the ballet's two acts does without it. It takes the play's wedding as the opportunity for an extended dance-within-dance sequence about ideal love that replaces the mechanicals' play-within-play of a comical-tragical love disaster. Act One, however, broadly follows the play's narrative with all its main elements – fairy quarrel, lovers' confusions, Bottom's transformation – plus the unusual feature of Titania's 'Cavalier', a dancing partner required because the quarrel means Oberon is not available. Like many Shakespeare ballets the narrative assumes knowledge of the play. Balanchine's aim, using minimal storytelling, is to depict the central elements of each situation – love quarrelling, happy, scorned, and distressed. At this the choreography is beautifully inventive, sometimes in unexpected ways. The most unusual choice is to use Mendelssohn's 'Nocturne', with its sublime quartet for horns and bassoons, for a *pas de deux* for Titania and Bottom-as-Ass, a bizarre combination of exalted music and comic-pathetic dance, to illustrate love as blind. At odds with the tone of the music, and drawing a veil over the element of humiliation in Oberon's design ('Wake when some vile thing is near' [2.2.33]), this is perhaps intended as comic irony. But while Mendelssohn's *Dream* music is supplemented from other sources, including the overture to his *Die erste Walpurgisnacht*, which gives an opportunity for some sinister violence (Hippolyta and hunting dogs), largely the darker sides of the play are kept at bay by choreography matched to music full of romantic feeling, but always mitigated by elegant restraint.

Frederick Ashton's *The Dream* was first staged as part of a triple bill to mark the quatercentenary of Shakespeare's birth in 1964, alongside a revival of Robert Helpmann's *Hamlet* (1942), with new material for Rudolf Nureyev as the Prince, and Kenneth MacMillan's *Images of Love*, nine cameos based on lines from Shakespeare (including four groups from *The Two Gentlemen of Verona*). Ashton's *Dream* is a slimmed-down epitome of the play, with no Theseus and Hippolyta, no forbidding of love, and no mechanicals' play. Oberon and Titania are central – their quarrel, the folly with Bottom, and their reconciliation. The vicissitudes of the lovers, with Oberon's device and Puck's erroneous execution, are a sub-plot. The period setting matches Mendelssohn's music: the fairies are not the international nature spirits of the play but Victorian English fairies, the corps de ballet halting occasionally in Taglioni-type tableaux which echo nineteenth-century ballet prints. Like Balanchine, Ashton assumes an audience that knows the play and concentrates on establishing mood and tone: witty, poised comedy for the (Victorian) lovers with their interchangeable affections, extravagant mimes of passion derived from Victorian melodrama, and conventional currency of romantic ballet choreography comically reversed; broader comedy for Bottom-as-Ass, dancing in block shoes for hooves to Mendelssohn's imitation of his donkey braying. The climax of the drama is a sublime reconciliation of Oberon and Titania, for which Ashton uses Mendelssohn's 'Nocturne' more straightforwardly, with choreography romantic and exalted to complement the comedy of love. The Fairy King and Queen end *The Dream* with mutuality in tenderness and a new awakening to love through conflicts and follies overcome.

Jean-Christophe Maillot's *Le Songe* (2005) is a full-length narrative version which uses Mendelssohn (for Athenians) supplemented by Daniel Teruggi (electronic, for fairies) and Bertrand Maillot (percussion plus, for artisans), differentiating the dramatic groups by music, choreography and costume as Shakespeare does by style. Though the additions to Mendelssohn mean Maillot does not use his different motifs for the different groups (the lovers, for example, dance to the fairy woodwind chords), he is consistently sensitive to the basic expressive character of the music. But Maillot's is a different dream. His whole reading of the play is sexualized, especially in his presentation of the fairies. Costumes for Oberon and Titania emphasizing their sexuality are matched by their choreography, especially in a final duet in which semi-suppressed violence is erotic, as is their quarrel – the page a girl, Oberon's interest in her sexual. Maillot manages not only to deliver all the main narrative elements but also to express a view of their central content – wonderfully inventive choreography, witty but also imaginatively sensitive in expressing the joy in each other and anguish at parental opposition of Hermia and Lysander, the distress of Helena, Theseus divided between support for social order and sympathy for young love; and all with full regard to the internal dynamics of choreography that makes sense as pure dance. The result is dance that both expresses narrative and character and is beautiful in itself.

Though not all aspects are equally successful (the play of Pyramus and Thisbe is truly tedious and not at all brief), overall it is a triumph of narrative ballet.

Other versions of the play that have proved durable in the repertoire of various companies include the great Shakespearean choreographer John Neumeier's (1977), in which the action is a dream of Hippolyta's the night before her marriage to Theseus. Mendelssohn is supplemented by György Ligeti for the fairies and orchestrated barrel organ music for the mechanicals, contrasts of musical style matched by distinct modes of choreography and costume. Heinz Spoerli (1976), for which Mendelssohn is supplemented by Philip Glass for fairies and Steve Reich for mechanicals, has, in his latest revision (1998), actors playing stagehands who interrupt to compound the confusion of identities. A score by Elvis Costello for choreography by Mauro Bigonzetti (2000), which follows the play's action in detail, likewise distinguishes in style between the different groups of characters – orchestral for aristocrats, swing for fairies, folk for mechanicals, mixing these modes as the characters become entwined. For David Nixon's version for Northern Ballet (2003) Mendelssohn is supplemented by Brahms, and the performance (in rich colours) is set within a frame which applies it to real life – the activities of a ballet company (in black and white) on an overnight train journey. A version by Michel Kelemenis for Ballet de Genève (2013) indicates the power of the play continually to generate creative re-readings: using intense bright-coloured shimmering costume fabrics, on a bare stage with only a few striking props, and thereby throwing all the attention onto semi-abstract movement, Kelemenis retains the main areas of fairies, lovers, and artisans, for dances that attempt to recreate the emotions with which the play deals without a narrative framework. Probably the weirdest experimental version is that of the Lindsay Kemp Dance Company (1985), filmed by Celestino Coronado (director of the so-called 'Naked *Hamlet*'), using Mendelssohn's music in parts. Jack Birkett as a silver-wigged Titania sets a keynote of camp transformations. Other creator-performers of the period with whom Kemp is associated – David Bowie, Kate Bush, Derek Jarman – suggest the flavour. Looking for sex in Shakespeare, Kemp is not the first or the last choreographer to find it in *A Midsummer Night's Dream*, but he finds it in ways all his own.

Romeo and Juliet

Most versions of *A Midsummer Night's Dream* use Mendelssohn, sometimes complemented with twentieth- and twenty-first century soundscapes and modern and contemporary styles of dancing and music-theatre. Whatever their bases in classical dance, most current versions of *Romeo and Juliet* use what has become one of the most successful modern ballet scores, and are therefore based in a twentieth-century soundscape with a Tchaikovskian background that profoundly affects their emotional character.

Leonid Lavrovsky's choreography (1940) to Prokofiev's 1935 score was not the ballet's first (by Ivo Psota, 1938), but it was the version that established the work in the theatre. (What the Lavrovsky choreography is, is open to question. The following discussion is based, not on the abbreviated version recorded in the 1954 film, but on the current Mariinsky production, assuming that this is closer to the work's original theatrical form.) Soviet in its social emphasis, this aspect of the choreography now carries no great dramatic weight: the violence and mimes of family hatred and rivalry are too plainly conventional. The street scenes, however, not only emphasize the feud but also, in brightly coloured and exuberant dance equivalents of Mercutio's zestful wit, present the straightforward pleasures of life that the feud destroys. While diminishing the roles of the Nurse and Friar Laurence, and so presenting the lovers as more isolated, and showing the circumstances driving them towards death only selectively, the narrative does maintain elements of the 'star-cross'd' plot: in particular the crucial spring of disaster – the killing of Mercutio – results from Romeo's attempt to stop the duel with Tybalt. There are also significant changes – no curse of Mercutio, for example – a key moment, drawing together the feud and the fates, and fulfilled in the denouement. The sense of a malign fate that the play so often enforces is, however, powerfully generated by Prokofiev's score: even movements most exuberant with the idealism of young love are weighted by melodic contour, harmony, or orchestration with an undertow of melancholy, which Lavrovsky enforces with details of the action – as when, before the wedding, Romeo examines with horrified fascination the skull on Laurence's writing desk.

Despite its contextual emphases, much of the power of Lavrovsky's choreography derives from the presentation of the lovers – the balcony scene, the wedding scene, the scene in Juliet's bedroom, the scene in the tomb. The wedding is indicative: by no means purely narrative, but – surprisingly in the Soviet context – taking a key from the play's imagery of love as sacred, it suggests what marriage means to the lovers. Their approach to the sacrament, echoing each other in steps suggesting awe and tenderness, establishes quite as much as the more exuberant and (chaste and child-like) erotic balcony scene the exalted character of what is destroyed. The beauty here of Juliet's apparently unsupported balances, and the sense of emotional poise they give, mean there is nothing that could possibly earn Laurence's warning, 'Wisely and slow' (2.3.90).

This presentation of the lovers reaches an apogee in the tomb scene. Prokofiev's first scenario proposed an ending in which they evade death and are happily united – perhaps feeling that socialist art should end with uplift, perhaps that a ballet might not end effectively in dancing with a 'dead' body. This problem is magnificently addressed by Lavrovsky in a single dramatic movement: raising Juliet's inert body straight above his head, then supporting the upper body with the right arm only, Romeo allows the lower body to sink so that it points straight to the ground. The final posture, a sort of elevated *pietà*, is extreme, and the way it is achieved so evidently on an edge of possibility, that the effect is of grief so devastating as to defy human limitations. It is a miracle of expressivity. A sudden appearance of Capulet and Montague and perfunctory reconciliation of feuding fathers does nothing to turn attention to any supposed healing of society. The Soviet social emphasis of the choreography remains to the end theoretical.

Among multiple competing versions the one that has most established itself as an alternative to Lavrovsky, overtly concentrated on the lovers, is that of Kenneth MacMillan (1965). Though the lovers are central, MacMillan was, like Shakespeare, a professional working with what is prescribed by the structure of a company: with any full-length work there must be roles for the corps de ballet. As with Shakespeare's fixed number of boys, the need for a Clown's part, and so on, the choreographer must put required crowd scenes to creative use. MacMillan's solution is to use the on-the-street dances as a bridge to the greater stylization of classical choreography for the lovers: only Juliet and her friends dance on pointe; only Romeo and his friends dance in men's ballet shoes. Low heels for women and boots for men mean that elsewhere the choreographic mode is closer to that of modern dance. Techniques from the Russian Imperial Ballet are democratically modified for the Age of the Beatles. It is a kind of balletic *verismo*. Realist, relative to the greater stylization it incorporates and supersedes, it provides a context in which the lovers stand out choreographically.

The lovers apart, MacMillan's most marked scenes are for the Capulet ball – group dances implying violence (march-like formations) and gender hierarchy (tableaux, with men upright and women kneeling) to define the sinister context Juliet is impelled to escape; and for Mercutio – dances of jesting wit to characterize the pleasant but ordinary world Romeo chooses to leave. These are the worlds of the play in dance equivalents. MacMillan also incorporates Mercutio's crucial curse, but otherwise minimizes narrative to concentrate on the lovers' experiences.

Like Lavrovsky, MacMillan gives Juliet an extended duet with Paris in apparent submission to the arranged marriage – characterizing the trauma of heroic isolation and the erotic intrusion into her union with Romeo through frozen upright stances, supported by Paris but never relaxing into him, which take their meaning in part from the contrast with her dances with Romeo. In the lovers' duets, the balcony and bedroom scenes, highly original lifts, throws, and other experiments that expand classical dance vocabulary, apparently to a limit of possibility, embody the extraordinariness, the breaching of limitation, that the lovers experience. The tomb scene is likewise a climax of invention that addresses in a different way Prokofiev's problem of the dance with the 'dead': Romeo's agony is depicted by having him hurl and fling Juliet's inert body into postures that recall the choreography of their love scenes.

Jean-Christophe Maillot's version (1996) is not set in the Renaissance. Bare sets, plain costumes, and stylized fights give no sense of time or place. It is then and now, one of several versions for 'today'. There are no rival families: the antagonisms are simply givens, a potential for violence always present. There are no early modern gender divisions: women participate in the violence equally with men. Crucially, unlike the other choreographers,

Maillot gives a central place to Laurence, who is not a friar but (less clearly placed in historical period) a priest. The drama proceeds from his agonies at society's violence, which are presented as a kind of crucifixion, generalizing the conflicts to represent all forms of hatred and violence. Intervening in the fights, he assumes responsibility for the general conduct of society as well as for the specific narrative of Romeo and Juliet. The tragedy is that of a will towards good that is powerless, or that – as Romeo, attempting to stop the duel with Tybalt, causes Mercutio's death – produces even greater evil.

Maillot's scenario and dramaturgy produce a powerful sense of tragic context. This is played out against the bawdy comedy of the Nurse and Mercutio, and the complementary formality, orthodoxy, and authority embodied in Lady Capulet, the only central character who consistently dances on pointe. When not on public display, venturing outside the conventions of her social position, like the young women in the streets Juliet dances in flat pumps. The clash of choreographic styles is indicative of Maillot's main focus – the convention-breaking experience of the lovers: the balcony scene conveying, in leaps, throws, and swirls, visionary joy – ideal forms of the wildness, tenderness, and reverence for the astonishing other of mutual adolescent erotic discovery; the bedroom and death scenes conveying a complementary agony at the brevity of joy and the power of violence that engulfs it. The contrast is encapsulated in a powerful emblem of love and despair: attempting to revive the supposed dead Juliet with a kiss, through his lips alone Romeo appears to resurrect her, raising her whole supine upper body by the force of his desire to infuse it with life. 'Ah, dear Juliet, / Why art thou yet so fair?' (5.3.101–2): agonizing for the audience that Romeo in effect sees that Juliet is alive, but cannot conceive the meaning of what he sees. Like Lavrovksy's 'pietà', Maillot's emblematic kiss is a magnificent example of Shakespeare-without-words equivalence.

In Angelin Preljocaj's version (1990, revised 2015), the most modern dance and least balletic to use Prokofiev, and even more emphatically for 'today', the feuding families are transformed into a ruling elite (to which Juliet belongs, and which keeps order with a brutal militia led by Tybalt), and an on-the-streets underclass (which includes Romeo). This is the East European totalitarianism of Preljocaj's family background. There are two Nurses, obverse duplicates of each other in costume and choreography, whose rigid movements, suggesting doll-like automata, parallel the quasi-military formalities of the ruling elite and contrast with the flexibility and fluidity of the underclass. There is no older generation, no Paris, which removes one catalyst of disaster, and no revenge for the killing of Mercutio, which removes the other. Though there is, therefore, no narrative need for Juliet's feigned death, this is nevertheless included. While Juliet's gym shoes and prominently nippled bra do not change her characterization as much as Romeo's murder of an elite-class guard with a cut-throat razor changes his, overall the differences in setting, narrative, characters, and characterization use selected elements of the play to create a tragedy of modern love that finally feels quite unlike the original.

In another recreation of emphatic contemporaneity, but differently experimental, Mauro Bigonzetti (2006) concentrates largely without narrative and without individual characters on the emotions to which narrative and character give rise. Romeo- and Juliet-type characters appear sometimes individually, sometimes in multiple forms, in costumes that suggest motorcycle gear-cum-sports armour (helmets, protective pads), to point contemporary relevance and a positive view of the excitements of risk-taking. One peculiarity is that the helmets are often worn upturned on a foot: what should be protective becomes a source of risk, or a source of instability in which the dancer strives for balance. While Bigonzetti foregrounds violence, sometimes apparently implying that violence (the life of risk at top speed) is an erotic stimulus, a lot of the choreography is romantic-erotic. A quasi-balcony scene duet in a wind machine (wind for speed) is beautiful and sensuous. A later scene of duets for several couples in sequence (as it were, a bedroom scene, after the violent deaths) gives a more extended presentation of the erotic, responsive to the varied implications of Prokofiev's score, from tenderness to ecstasy. Weirdly unlike Shakespeare though some of this is, despite the near absence of narrative, and beneath the superficial clash of styles, this is a real creative interaction with the play.

Mats Ek aims for contemporaneity by another route. Set to music arranged from Tchaikovsky, as its title implies, Ek's *Juliet and Romeo* (2013) redirects attention to the female perspective. Ek explains that he was prompted to think afresh about the play, and about how a small event can prompt social change, by the 2010 suicide of a Tunisian street-seller that precipitated the 'Arab Spring' movements for greater democracy in the Middle East – though this is not specifically implied in the presentation, except insofar as the contextual violence is presented not in terms of a family feud but of political turmoil: have-not youth on the streets confront flailing authority (the Prince) and haves (Capulets) who police their precinct on Segways. The topical issue Ek overtly foregrounds is that of forced marriage: when Juliet refuses, her death, directed by her father, is an 'honour' killing. Into this unusual context Ek introduces some clichés of later twentieth-century *Romeos*: as in Franco Zeffirelli's 1968 film (and many presentations thereafter) Mercutio is gay, and Lady Capulet involved in a sexual relationship with Tybalt. Ek follows some of the play's narrative structure, but with no marriage to Juliet, no challenge to Romeo by Tybalt, no intervention by Romeo in a Tybalt-Mercutio fight, and a choreography of the bedroom scene which, in keeping with the anti-romantic style, is low-key, the focus is consistently deflected from love to parental tyranny and forced marriage. The lovers draw the society together at the end in symbolic solidarity with their sacrifice, but the thematic reorientation makes it difficult to feel much for what has been lost. Straining for contemporaneity drains the work of natural feeling.

There have been many other versions, some historic – by Bronislava Nijinska for the Ballets Russes (1926), with music by Constant Lambert and designs by Max Ernst and Joan Miró; by Serge Lifar, in a one-act version to the Tchaikovsky Fantasy Overture (1942); and a one-act version by the English choreographer Antony Tudor (1943), with Jerome Robbins (later the choreographer of *West Side Story*) in the cast, to music by Delius (partly from his opera *A Village Romeo and Juliet*). In this version, as in Garrick's (1748), and in Baz Luhrmann's film (1995), Juliet revives before Romeo dies – an alternative way of addressing the problem of dance with a 'dead' body. Other still-current versions to the Prokofiev score include those by Frederick Ashton for Danish National Ballet (1955; unlike other Western choreographers, Ashton was not influenced by Lavrovsky, whose version he had not seen); John Cranko (1958, revised 1962), which follows the play closely, showing how important is the hurtling pace and the narrative pattern by which positive movement is immediately counteracted by negative; Maurice Béjart

(1966, revised 1972), who uses the dramatic symphony of Berlioz, setting the narrative within a 'make love not war' frame that applies the work to contemporary student protest movements; John Neumeier (1971), the first of several innovative treatments of Shakespeare, with eager adolescent central figures, perhaps influenced by Franco Zeffirelli's then-recent film; Rudolf Nureyev (1977), with a particularly strong characterization of Juliet, including scenes in which she confronts Romeo after the death of Tybalt, and chooses between life (the sleeping potion, offered by the Ghost of Mercutio) and death (a knife offered by the Ghost of Tybalt); Peter Martins (2007), for New York City Ballet; Krzysztof Pastor (2008), with each of its three acts set in a different problematic era of twentieth-century Italian politics (1930s, Mussolini; 1970s, Red Brigades; 1990s, Berlusconi); Alexei Ratmansky (2011), who (like Tudor) allows Juliet to revive before Romeo dies, and also includes Shakespeare's reconciliation of the families. More experimental versions include those of Mark Morris (2008), to the rediscovered original Prokofiev score, with its happy ending, given typical Morris gender twists, with a female Mercutio and Tybalt; a hip hop version with choreography by Sébastien Lefrançois to music by Laurent Couson (2008); versions using Berlioz by Sasha Waltz (2007) and Thierry Malandin (2010); and a version by the Rasta Thomas Dance Company (Rasta Thomas of 'Bad Boys of Dance'), with choreography by Adrienne Canterna (2015) and a sound track ranging from Vivaldi to Lady Gaga. For dance the subject is evidently inexhaustible.

Hamlet and *Othello*

From *Giselle* to *Swan Lake* and beyond, supernatural beings, ideal love and erotic trauma have been the stuff of ballet. Clearly, in this context, even independent of the tempting scores of Mendelssohn and Prokofiev, *A Midsummer Night's Dream* and *Romeo and Juliet* present alluring subjects. Many other Shakespeare plays have been used as the basis for ballets, sometimes with scores that may have played a part in prompting the choice (Tchaikovsky's *Hamlet* overture, or his symphonic fantasia, *The Tempest*; the incidental music for *The Tempest* of Sibelius); but few of these ballets have established themselves in the repertoire – though in some cases (most obviously John Neumeier's *Othello* [1985]) this may be only because no recording has yet been made which would give the work a form of currency now almost usual for major productions.

Of various *Hamlets*, some, like Robert Helpmann's (1942, 1964), are epitomes, or concentrate on some single aspect of the play, including Ashton's *Hamlet Preludes* (1977), to Liszt's symphonic poem *Hamlet*; MacMillan's *Sea of Troubles* (1977, 1992), to Martinů and Webern; and Mauro Bigonzetti's *ToBeOrNotToBe* (2004), to Purcell, Bach, and Handel. Full-length versions include those of Béjart (1989), to Duke Ellington and Purcell; Svetlana Voskresenskaya (Moscow, 1991), to Shostakovich; Kevin O'Day (Stuttgart, 2008), to a commissioned score by John King; and David Nixon with Patricia Doyle (Northern Ballet, 2011), to a commissioned score by Philip Feeney, set in a Nazi-occupied Paris of tyranny and collaboration. The choreography by Stephen Mills to Philip Glass, devised for Ballet Austin (2000) and presented by various American companies, seems most to have established itself in the repertoire. But *Hamlet* is a play that has both allured and resisted dance: the clear successes have concentrated on some limited aspect of the play, as with the *Hamlet* in John Neumeier's triple bill, *Shakespeare Dances* (2013, with *As You Like It*, and *Twelfth Night*). These short ballets, rather than presenting the plays, investigate creating play-based dance: they indicate how Neumeier's idea of creative interaction works, by focusing on theme, on links between music and words, on cameos epitomizing fundamental tones, or on other elements of a play especially amenable to being danced – which, with his *Hamlet* (a re-working of three earlier versions [1976, 1985, 1997]), are narrative backgrounds: the pre-play relations of Hamlet and Ophelia and (as in Saxo Grammaticus) of Gertrude with Claudius before her marriage to Hamlet père.

One ballet based on a tragedy that has established a place in the international repertoire is José Limón's *The Moor's Pavan* (1949). To music adapted from Purcell, this is a short work for four dancers – Othello and Desdemona, Iago and Emilia – and a handkerchief. It has no plot, simply an action in which Othello is made jealous by the handkerchief stolen by Emilia and manipulated by Iago. The engagements prompted are more straightforward than those of the play – pity for Othello and Desdemona as victims of a process made present only in outline: love corrupted by insinuation leads through suspicion to conviction of betrayal. All four characters remain on stage throughout, and act to each other, not the audience, heightening the claustrophobic trajectory towards murder. Dancing in pairs shows alliances created and trust corrupted – archetypal situations emphasized by the formal patterns of the stately Renaissance dance mode (pavan) from which the work begins. Drawing on ballet, modern dance, Renaissance dance, and mime, the combination of formal group movement and expressive individual gesture, eschewing plot, gives the piece a strongly marked character quite unlike that of other Shakespeare ballets.

Lar Lubovitch's *Othello* (1997), a full-length narrative ballet to a score by Elliot Goldenthal, is quite different. All the main characters of the play are included, with an enlarged role for Bianca, as an incarnation of generalized erotic feeling, the opposite of Desdemona's focused personal love. Like Verdi, Lubovitch establishes the love that is to be destroyed in an extended duet for Othello and Desdemona, and (also like Verdi, and unlike the Mexican-American Limón) he plays down the issue of race. Iago's motives, at first confined to resentment at being passed over for promotion combined with unfocused psychotic violence (evident in his treatment of Emilia), do not include racial animus. The suggestions that prompt Othello's jealousy are insinuated in a context of sexual violence by the corps de ballet, a tarantella led by Bianca: a general atmosphere of release in Cyprus after the formality of Venice implies that Othello's descent into destructive passion is a particular instance of a general malaise.

While this simplifies, in another area the ballet brings out a subtext of the play. Cassio's supposed dream recounted by Iago, though it describes a heterosexual fantasy, is a vividly imagined account of homosexual actions which can be interpreted as implying a submerged current in Iago's motive-hunting and pleasure in destroying Othello's love for Desdemona. In Lubovitch's ballet a video backdrop showing Cassio making love to Desdemona conveys Iago's insinuations to Othello. Iago's gestures with the watching Othello parallel Cassio's with Desdemona, reversing the process of the play dream: Iago enforces his fantasy of heterosexual sex by enacting it in actual endearments with Othello. Some of the ballet's most inventive choreography may be seen as developing this. In a duet between the two men, Iago seduces (gestures of submission), leads (Othello mirrors his movements and gestures), and dominates Othello (on his shoulder, balancing in tableau; on his back, gripping with spider-like legs). Is this interpretative, developing submerged desires implied by the dream-enactment? In the unfixed signification of dance, that is left to the audience.

Present and future – with pre-echoes

Amid the second wave of modern feminism, and in the wake of Franco Zeffirelli's film (1967), John Cranko saw the contemporary gender-trouble potential of *The Taming of the Shrew* (1969, to Domenico Scarlatti arranged by Karl-Heinz Stolze), and that the play also presented Odette/Odile (from *Swan Lake*) dance roles that revised ballet gender issues in a modern way – Bianca as sweet-to-saccharine Odette, the superseded romantic-passive; Kate as comic-athletic Odile, a heroine for the 1960s. Jean-Christophe Maillot returned to the play, using music by Shostakovich (mainly from his satirical operetta, *Moskva Cheryomushki*), for one of several works composed for the anniversary year of 2014 (Bolshoi Ballet). Other 2014 anniversary works turned to the late plays, including Christopher Wheeldon's *The Winter's Tale* for the Royal Ballet. Despite Glen Tetley's full-length version for Ballet Rambert (1979) and Nureyev's epitome for the Royal Ballet (1982), with *The Tempest* it is as though choreographers have only lately seen that the play's magic, supernatural beings, ideal love, and comic artisans give it central elements in common with *A Midsummer Night's Dream*, and that it is a work peculiarly open to investigation by different readings and to the kind of archetypal presentation (the father, the lovers, the air, the earth) that suits dance. Crystal Pite's *The Tempest Replica* (2011) is a mixture of abstract dance and narrative with storyboards. Described as 'based on motifs from *The Tempest*', it is concerned with Prospero's relationships with the other main characters and his choice of love over power and revenge – though no summary could do justice to its various weirdnesses of mode and form. More straightforward is Alexei Ratmansky's one-act version for American Ballet Theater (2013), to the incidental music for the play by Sibelius. Like Pite's version, Krzysztof Pastor's anniversary offering for Dutch National Ballet (2014), a collaboration with the video artist Sherin Neshat, for which sixteenth- and seventeenth-century English music (Tallis to Purcell) are combined with the daf (Iranian frame drum), mixes modes in a postmodern kind of way. It investigates the play's back-story: Prospero's restraint of Ferdinand's pursuit of Miranda in the play is replicated in an earlier relationship with Caliban. He is a father who cannot let go. A version by David Bintley for the Birmingham Royal Ballet for 2016, with a commissioned score by the Scottish composer Sally Beamish (at the time of writing still under construction) will be more in the mode of Ratmansky than Pite or Pastor. Bintley's earlier *The Shakespeare Suite* (1999), eight cameos to Duke Ellington and Billy Strayhorn, gives the choreographic idea.

The potential for drama that Kenneth MacMillan exploited briefly in *Images of Love* has been more fully developed in two more anniversary works: *Sonett* by Christian Spuck (2014, Zurich Ballet) uses Sonnets 20, 66, 144 and 147 to music by Philip Glass; *Wink*, by Jessica Lang, a new work based on the poems for Birmingham Royal Ballet (2016), will experiment with music by Jakub Ciupiński for the electro-acoustic theremin. Polish National Ballet will complete a 2014/16 Festival of Shakespeare (including Neumeier's *Dream*, Cranko's *Shrew*, and Pastor's *Tempest*) with a new full-length *Hamlet* by Jacek Tyski.

There are ballets based on Dante and Milton, Tolstoy and Proust, but no writer has contributed to dance like Shakespeare. The history of Shakespeare in modern classical dance begins, like much else about ballet, with Marius Petipa – a staging of *A Midsummer Night's Dream* to Mendelssohn in St Petersburg (1876), the choreography for which is lost. Within the conventions this model established, only a limited range of Shakespeare's plays were likely to be attempted, but, as classical ballet absorbed more from other modes of modern dance, so the potential Shakespearean repertoire enlarged. Now even a *King Lear* has been attempted (Igor Dobrovolskiy, dramaturge Sharon Pollock, to Shostakovich, Atlantic Ballet Theatre of Canada, 2008). That the anniversaries of 2014 and 2016 should prompt a range of new works, some based on unusual Shakespeare sources, many experimenting with new styles of dance and new mixtures of dance, music, and drama, suggests that the future of creative experiment in dance theatre may be no less engaged with Shakespeare than its past.

5

Shakespeare and Opera

Penny Gay

Towards the end of the sixteenth century, there was an interesting, and perhaps inevitable, confluence of High Renaissance art forms. Just as Shakespeare began writing his psychologically complex plays in England, the first identifiable operas were being performed in Italy at the courts of Florence and Mantua. The achievements of Claudio Monteverdi – with *Orfeo* in 1607, and, later, *L'incoronazione di Poppea* (Venice, 1642), character-driven dramas based on fluid musical narrative and complex characterization – ensure that his operas are still widely performed today, and considered to be humanist masterpieces in the same way that Shakespeare's plays are.

This new musical art form was making its influence felt in England just as the Puritans were seeking to shut down the spoken-drama playhouses as fomenters of immorality. During this period of public repression, some private houses – for example, that of the courtier and playwright Sir William Davenant – were able to offer moralizing representations of historical subjects, 'writ in verse and performed in recitative music. The original of the music, and of the scenes which adorned this work', Davenant had, Dryden tells us, 'from the Italian operas' (Dryden, *Essay of Heroic Plays*); such entertainments were performed in purpose-built, small indoor theatres drawing on the spectacular tradition of the court masque. The diarist John Evelyn saw 'a new opera, after the Italian way, in recitative music and scenes' in 1659 in London. When public theatre was once again permitted, after the restoration of King Charles II, and the 'old plays' were being revived, an 'operatic' aesthetic was imposed on those plays whose themes were tragic or moralizing: they now seemed to need the heightened effect of music. This consisted not simply of incidental songs – many Shakespearean comedies came already equipped with these – but moments of full-scale operatic spectacle.

Davenant was one of the two courtiers who were given the rights by the king to produce the old plays, including those of Shakespeare; but the works needed to be 'reformed and made fit' for a new audience who had a veneer of European sophistication due to the long exile of the court in France. This often meant 'correcting' Shakespeare's language to a more even style, and providing extra plot and characters to create the symmetries and contrasts admired by neo-Classical theory. At the same time, the spectacle of scenery and 'machines', with extensive music, was demanded, despite obvious incongruities with the narrative. Davenant began this process, but the most successful operatic versions of his revisions of old plays were made after his death in 1668.

The first was *Macbeth*. Davenant's revision had greatly increased the roles of Macduff and his Lady, supplying a virtuous, unambitious, moralizing couple to contrast with the villainous Macbeths. That satisfied neo-Classical theorists. But for those who demanded spectacle and music, the Witches were the main attraction, at first played by men as a sort of unearthly chorus-line in drag. John Downes reported on the long-lasting success of this adaptation in *Roscius Anglicanus* (1708):

> The tragedy of *Macbeth*, altered by Sir William Davenant; being dressed in all its finery, as new clothes, new scenes, machines, as flyings for the witches; with all the singing and dancing in it: the first composed by Mr. Lock, the other by Mr. Channell and Mr. Joseph Priest; it being all excellently performed, being in the nature of an opera, it recompensed double the expense; it proves still a lasting play.

The second was a rewriting of *The Tempest*, this time in collaboration with Dryden. Classical symmetry demanded that Miranda, the girl who had never seen a boy, should have an equivalent (also living on the island!) in Hippolito, a boy who had never seen a girl – and the plot needed to be revised to provide an extra girl (Miranda's sister Dorinda), as Miranda is spoken for. Once again it was the supernatural elements that attracted an operatic upgrade. Downes gives details:

The year after in 1673, *The Tempest, or the Enchanted Island*, made into an opera by Mr. Shadwell, having all new in it; as scenes, machines ... all things performed in it so admirably well, that not any succeeding opera got more money.

Shadwell's opening stage directions elaborate on the substantial orchestra required to accompany the supernatural spectacles: a 'band, of twenty-four violins, with the harpsicals and theorbos which accompany the voices, are placed between the pit and the stage'. (Wind and brass were added by the end of the seventeenth century.) A masque of Neptune and Amphitrite ends the play, with gods drawn in a chariot by sea-horses, and a dance of twelve Tritons; then the 'scene changes to the rising sun, and a number of aerial spirits in the air, Ariel flying from the sun, advances towards the pit', where he sings 'Where the Bee Sucks', while 'hovering in the air'. The music was once again by Matthew Locke.

A final popular example of these first Shakespeare 'operas' is *The Fairy Queen*, Henry Purcell's 1693 spin-off from *A Midsummer Night's Dream*. While a version of Shakespeare's text was spoken by actors, what made the performance spectacular were the 'entries' at the end of Acts 2, 3, 4 and 5, in which a group of singers and dancers performed masques in elaborately-constructed and changing scenery, with very little to do with the action of the play. Fauns, Dryads and Naiades, and a pastoral duet for Coridon and Mopsa, follow Act 3; after Act 4, a garden of fountains, with Apollo and the Four Seasons, Juno and her peacocks and a Chinese garden. A grand dance of 'Chineses' ended the show. Downes reports that it was 'excellently performed, chiefly the instrumental and vocal part composed by the said Mr. Purcell, and dances by Mr. Priest. The court and town were wonderfully satisfied with it; but the expenses in setting it out being so great, the company got very little by it.'

Although other Shakespeare plays were 'operatized' in similar fashion with inserted masques at the end of the seventeenth century (Gildon's *Measure for Measure*, 1695; Lansdowne's *Jew of Venice*, 1701), the inorganic and expensive nature of the operatic extras soon led to these novelties being dropped. Only *Macbeth* and *The Tempest* remained 'in the nature of an opera' in the theatrical repertoire for some decades to come – though the very notion of English opera was challenged by the arrival, in the first decade of the 1700s, of the Italian Opera at its own house in the Haymarket, to which fashionable society thronged.

Two strands in the adaptation of the Shakespearean text were enormously influential in later productions: using operatic conventions to depict otherworldly or non-human characters, and expanding aesthetic variety, via spectacle and music, in plays considered to be old-fashioned and provincial. In the early eighteenth century a popular example is David Garrick's *The Fairies* (1755), a short adaptation of *A Midsummer Night's Dream* which cuts all the 'Hard-handed men' material, including 'Pyramus and Thisbe', in order to provide a pleasing light-opera spectacle of lovers and fairies. The music was by J. C. Smith; it was welcomed by at least one reviewer as 'a laudable attempt to encourage native musical productions'. Shakespeare's lines were spoken, then the same actor burst into an 'Air' vaguely relevant to the situation; there were twenty-seven songs in all. (This is not unlike the model used so successfully by Gilbert and Sullivan in the late nineteenth century.) In 1756 Garrick did the same thing with *The Tempest*, advertised as an 'Opera' on its printed title page, getting rid of many of Dryden's classicizing excrescences and adding thirty-two songs, duets, and trios by Smith. Where the Elizabethans and Jacobeans were content to accept all sorts of unlikely happenings on stage, with only the power of Shakespeare's words to support them, the more 'rational' later-seventeenth and eighteenth centuries, influenced by French neo-Classical aesthetic theory, required these moments and characters to be framed by a different genre: music, the inexplicable and non-rational form that appeals directly to our emotions.

In the Europe of Mozart's day, Shakespeare's comedies had some success in operatic adaptation. In 1786 Stephen Storace (an Englishman living in Vienna, and a close friend of Mozart) wrote a delightful *The Comedy of Errors*, titled *Gli Equivoci*, with a libretto by Lorenzo Da Ponte, of which the singer Michael Kelly remarked that it 'retained all the main incidents and characters of our immortal bard'. This opera by an Englishman in the Italian comic tradition was not produced in England – perhaps because by then the English public were too wedded to the light-opera mode, with spoken dialogue, dance, and stage spectacle.

One of the greatest successes on the English stage in the early nineteenth century was the series of elaborate quasi-operatic Shakespeare productions under the entrepreneurship of Frederick Reynolds at Covent Garden (still technically a playhouse, not an opera-house). Reynolds began with *A Midsummer Night's Dream* in 1816, with song and dance mostly undertaken by the play's characters, including a 'Fairy ballet'. The 'opera' cuts the play's final scene for the fairies, and substitutes a grand pageant of Theseus' triumph. Reynolds then attempted to reproduce this success with *The Comedy of Errors* in 1819, which included many songs from other Shakespeare plays not often performed. This was successfully revived for some years; as was *Twelfth Night* in 1820 on the same model: 'interspersed with song, glees, and duets, taken from the German and English masters' and adapted by theatre composer Henry Bishop. Most popular was Reynolds's *The Merry Wives of Windsor* at Drury Lane in 1824, with admirable performances by singer-actors such as John Braham, Miss Stephens and Mme Vestris; this version continued to be performed well into the later nineteenth century.

As the above account shows, it was mostly the comedies that were subject to operatic treatment in England. By the early nineteenth century on the Continent, however, a burgeoning taste for a Romantic and melodramatic aesthetic saw the Shakespearean text providing libretti for full-scale grand opera, which was now a dominant artistic genre throughout Europe – and not dependent on language so much as on its emotive musical equivalent.

Gioachino Rossini was first off the rank with his *Otello* of 1816: much of the plot is re-shaped to fit Italian opera conventions, but in Act 3, following Shakespeare closely, Desdemona sings a beautiful and dramatic Willow Song and prayer. She is stabbed, not smothered, by Otello. Vincenzo Bellini's *I Capuleti e i Montecchi* (1830) is more closely based on Matteo Bandello's original novella (Shakespeare's source for *Romeo and Juliet*) than on Shakespeare's play, though the names of the characters may encourage audiences to expect a close poetic parallel. Hector Berlioz, a Shakespeare enthusiast, composed his own French libretto for *Béatrice et Bénédict* (1862), using heavily-cut dialogue from *Much Ado About Nothing*. But there is no Don John, no Dogberry, and no public rejection of Hero by Claudio: Berlioz's interest is all in the relationship between Beatrice and Benedict. It makes for a very lightweight (though lyrical) opera – more of a *divertissement* than a full adaptation. Without the terrible accusations of the church scene, and Beatrice's passionate demand 'Kill Claudio!', the lovers lack gravitas.

With the works of Giuseppe Verdi, serious operas based on Shakespeare's dramas became central in the cultural repertoire. His first was *Macbeth*, in 1847. 'The main roles of this opera are, and can only be, *three*: Macbeth, Lady Macbeth and the chorus of witches. The witches dominate the drama; everything stems from them – rude and gossipy in Act I, exalted and prophetic in Act III. They make up a real character, and one of the greatest importance': thus wrote Verdi to Escudier, his French publisher, as he worked on revisions for the French premiere in 1865. Verdi instinctively knew that the Witches in *Macbeth* were vital not only to the play's plot but also to its mood and ethos. He may have seen some version of the English 'operatic' rendition of the witches, traditional since Davenant's version, when he attended a production of the play in London in 1847; in some ways, what we hear of the witches in Verdi's choruses reflects this traditional conception of them. But a Romantic enthusiasm for the supernatural, ghosts, and dark forces not subject to Christian rule had begun to create a widespread desire to return to Shakespeare's original conception of these matters, and Verdi, who knew his Shakespeare well (in translation), aspired to write appropriately strange music within the parameters of the operatic choruses of his day. (He also added highly effective ballet music for the witches for the Paris version of 1865.)

Although Verdi's chorus of witches is female, the original text and the opera libretto both feature Banquo's line on his and Macbeth's first encounter with them: 'you should be women, / And yet your beards forbid me to interpret / That you are so' (1.3.45–7). This sexual ambiguity – or, rather, monstrousness – connects subliminally to a basic theme of the play: the natural world has turned on itself. Verdi chooses, like English producers of the stage play in the period, not to show the most shocking moment in Shakespeare's play, the murder of Lady Macduff and her children, but he ensures that it is referred to and becomes a vital element in the guilt of the protagonists – particularly Lady Macbeth. It is regrettable that nineteenth-century standards of decency presumably stopped Verdi from setting the Lady's spine-chilling invocation of the diabolic world when she hears of Duncan's imminent arrival:

> Come, you Spirits
> That tend on mortal thoughts, unsex me here,
> And fill me, from the crown to the toe, top-full
> Of direst cruelty!
>
> (1.5.39–42)

Verdi's retention of Lady Macbeth's womanliness creates a radical difference between play and opera. Of course Shakespeare was writing for a highly talented boy actor, Verdi for a *prima donna*. But there is more to it than mere casting issues. With the acceptance throughout Europe of adult actresses working on the professional theatre stage, roles were demanded and written for them of equal power and weight. The consequence was a deeper exploration of, among other things, the marital relationship. Lady Macbeth, in both Shakespeare and Verdi, is a monstrous figure, but in Verdi her unnatural personality is subsumed in her equal partnership in crime with her husband. For example, she sends Macbeth off in full knowledge that he will arrange the murder of Banquo; it is she who (in the 1865 revision) sings Macbeth's line from Act 3, Scene 2 of the play: 'La luce langue' – 'Light thickens'. Instead of Macbeth's poetic consciousness (an aspect of the Shakespearean text that keeps the audience in profound empathy with him) we have the Lady declaring, 'A new crime! It is necessary! ... Oh, voluptuous joy of the throne! Oh sceptre, thou art mine at last!' Verdi's Lady Macbeth conforms much more closely to the nineteenth-century type of the villainess. Her active involvement in Macbeth's crimes is further signalled in the duet (added in 1865) that closes Act 3, 'Hour of death and vengeance! ... The enterprise by crime must end, since with blood it was begun.'

Despite this apparent cognitive self-command, Lady Macbeth's sleepwalking scene is a brilliant setting by Verdi almost exactly as it was written by Shakespeare. The soprano's broken utterances, sighs and cries – a major musical development of the operatic convention of the mad scene – are the signs of 'a mind diseas'd' unable to 'Pluck from the memory a rooted sorrow' (5.3.40, 41). This scene is as powerful as the famous performances in the theatre by the great actress Sarah Siddons at the end of the eighteenth century. By contrast, Verdi does not give Macbeth the poetic soliloquies that

Shakespeare wrote. He had, arguably, other agendas relevant to a nineteenth-century Italian audience: to show the defeat of a tyrant, and an unequivocal restoration of national order.

Verdi's two late Shakespearean masterpieces, *Otello* (1887) and *Falstaff* (1893), confirmed his genius with the playwright's stories. Shakespeare's *Othello*, with its tale of domestic violence and racism, and its long list of aria-like public speeches, in many people's view works better as hyperbolic opera than it does as a too-painful play. The action of the opera, carefully filleted down by Verdi's librettist Arrigo Boito (in close collaboration with the composer) to Shakespeare's scenes on Cyprus, is most notable for its depiction of Iago, whose extraordinary Credo provides a kind of generalized motivation, largely missing from the play, for his vicious actions: 'I believe in a cruel God / who created me in his image / and who in fury I name'. This invokes nineteenth-century notions of the nihilist, alienated from society. Iago's music has a dry, almost conversational quality, as though he is concealing his inner self even from the audience, unlike Shakespeare's character who gleefully plays the Vice and demands the audience's admiration. Otello's music is more conventionally operatic, with arias and love duets; and for Desdemona there is (as in Rossini's much earlier opera) a heart-stoppingly beautiful Willow Song and prayer.

Verdi had for many years worked on the idea of making an opera out of *King Lear*, but it never came to fruition: *Otello* clearly shows that it might have been another extraordinary work mining the essence of Shakespeare's play and giving it a nineteenth-century resonance. *Falstaff*, by contrast, is a comedy, also devised with Boito as librettist, based on *The Merry Wives of Windsor* but incorporating some parts of *King Henry IV*, Parts 1 and 2, most notably Falstaff's 'Honour' monologue, now repositioned as a pub harangue in the context of how to get money by guile. The opera is a freer adaptation than *Otello*'s strict adherence to Shakespeare's plot, fast-moving and almost symphonic in its fleeting use of vocal and orchestral thematic figures. Its final fugal chorus, led by Falstaff, places him as a loveable force of nature, who not only celebrates the joys of food, wine, and love, but who also acknowledges a wry anti-authoritarian wisdom: 'Tutto nel mondo è burla' – 'Everything in the world is a joke'.

Other European composers had climbed onto the Shakespearean opera bandwagon in the mid-nineteenth century, unconstrained by the need to represent the whole text, but also happy to claim the Bard's stories as universally relevant. Taking the tragic high ground, Charles Gounod had a great success with his *Roméo et Juliette* (1867), focusing on the lovers and their ecstatic duets. As had been the practice in straight theatre productions since Garrick's day, the lovers have a final duet: Juliette awakens before Roméo dies in a scene that evokes the Romantic trope of the *Liebestod*, though their last united cry is the rather more conventional prayer 'Seigneur, Seigneur, pardonnez-nous!' Ambroise Thomas's *Hamlet* (1868) similarly follows Shakespeare quite closely, though with significant cuts to characters and scenes, until the last scene, at Ophelia's funeral, when Hamlet and Laertes fight; in Thomas's version Hamlet does not die, but becomes king after killing Claudius. This version of the play is based on Alexandre Dumas's French adaptation, and it conforms to the traditional decorums of the Comédie-Française, as well as those of grand opera. It concentrates on the four main characters: Hamlet (tenor), Ophélie (soprano), Claudius (bass), and Gertrude (mezzo-soprano), and their arias and duets. Hamlet sings his most famous soliloquy, 'Être ou ne pas être', just before the closet scene, during which he also rejects Ophelia, who consequently goes mad and drowns herself following a conventional nineteenth-century operatic mad scene, thus embodying the *femme fragile*, who cannot exist without the validation of her lover. (Polonius, a much-reduced figure in the opera, is not involved in the closet scene and does not die.)

In the rarer comic mode, Otto Nicolai's *Die lustigen Weiber von Windsor* (1849), a musically rich 'komische-fantastische Oper' (Nicolai's term) with some spoken dialogue, still keeps a place in the repertoire. Falstaff, Ford and the unsuccessful suitors are comic *opera buffa* roles. In the vein of romantic opera are the love scenes between Anna and Fenton, the 'ghost' and 'elf' music, and the famous musical impression of the moonrise that begins the final scene. Most interestingly, in this 'fairy' scene the *ingénue* Anne performs not the play's generic Fairy Queen but Titania, and her lover Fenton plays Oberon. Nicolai's opera premiered in Berlin only six years after a production of *A Midsummer Night's Dream* in the same city showcased Mendelssohn's complete incidental music for the first time. This demonstrates yet again the persistent power of Shakespeare's imagined fairy world from the *Dream*. In *The Merry Wives* (both play and opera), the bourgeois 'wives' of the story tap into, and make use of, the English folk-memory of the 'little people' that Shakespeare's play so richly embodies: they are uncanny, yet familiar, and they are there at the edge of every rural community's imagination.

In the tradition of the *singspiel*, and for comic and farcical effect that matches the Shakespearean text for genuine wit, the twentieth century produced some wonderful comic 'operas' (requiring lead singers with classical vocal training) in the new form of the American musical. Of the several hundred Shakespeare musicals produced around the world, *The Boys from Syracuse* (1938), one of the earliest, is a lively version of Shakespeare's farce-cum-romance *The Comedy of Errors*, with music by Richard Rodgers and lyrics by Lorenz Hart; the book, by George Abbot, is 'very much in the bawdy Shakespearean tradition' (according to a delighted Rodgers), focusing on the Dromio twins and the 'low' comedy. It has remained in the repertoire of musical theatre worldwide, as has the most popular example of the Shakespeare musical, the metatheatrical *Kiss Me, Kate* (1948, music and lyrics by Cole Porter, book by Sam and Bella Spewack). The story involves the production of a touring musical version of *The Taming of the Shrew*, the plot of which is echoed in the off-stage conflict between (and eventual reconciliation of) the show's director and star and his leading lady, who happens to be his ex-wife. Its musical styles are wide-ranging and involve a great deal of self-referential wit. Whether its romantic conclusion – a given in the mid-century American musical – is to an audience's satisfaction today, now that theatre companies are much more inclined to perform the original play's ending subversively, does not detract from the delightful theatricality of the whole piece. Frances Teague shrewdly comments that 'a musical that attends to Shakespeare is likely to attend to gender, class and race as well, but not in any solemn or profound way. The jokes are suggestive or vulgar, the music and dancing energetic and the principal barrier to success is too much respect for the original work.' It is easy to imagine Shakespeare approving this brave new world, among the many musical transformations of his plays over the centuries.

In the twentieth century's classical tradition, only Benjamin Britten's *A Midsummer Night's Dream* (1960), with a libretto drawn directly from

Shakespeare by Britten and Peter Pears, achieves the near-impossible task of a through-composed opera that maintains Shakespearean comedy's wit and verve. Britten's setting is replete with references to earlier operatic styles, including the mechanicals' Pyramus and Thisbe play as a nineteenth-century opera in miniature, complete with melodramatic deaths and a vocally ornate mad scene for Thisbe. The play's comedy is all the funnier for the extra layer of in-jokes about vocal styles and types: from Bottom's bully-boy bass to Flute's high tenor, with the quartet of lovers making up a standard nineteenth-century soprano, mezzo, tenor and baritone line-up. But again most interesting of all is the depiction of the fairies: Moth, Peaseblossom and their cohort are boy trebles, mischievous and playful; Puck is a spoken role that requires acrobatic skills, Titania a coloratura soprano, and Oberon a mysterious, powerful, otherworldly countertenor. Britten's admiration for Purcell (who wrote extensively for countertenor in the first period of 'Shakespeare operatized') here reaches across the centuries to enable English music gloriously to reclaim the greatest English playwright.

The most recently successful Shakespeare opera, Thomas Adès's *The Tempest* (2004), also offers an unworldly voice (a high soprano) for the role of Ariel, Prospero's fairy servant and magical enabler. The critic Adrian Streete comments that 'it is the element of fantasy that Adès's opera invokes, indeed that all the great Shakespearean operas manage to conjure, which sets it apart: Ariel's music is truly, as Ferdinand says, neither "I'th' air, or th'earth" [1.2.388] ... [it is] something strange, magical and slightly crazy'. The opera has a libretto by Meredith Oakes, in which Shakespeare's lines are shortened and re-written as rhyming or semi-rhyming couplets. Prospero's poetic musings at the end of the masque, for example, are rendered into the more easily singable:

> Our revels are ended
> Why do you stare?
> He's melted into air
> So cities will perish
> Palaces vanish
> The globe itself
> Dissolve away

Nothing stay
All will fade.

Prospero and Ariel might stand as allegorical figures for the twin underpinnings of successful Shakespearean opera. Prospero, despite his 'so potent art' (5.1.50), cannot provide the wedding masque for Miranda and Ferdinand, or indeed the tempest itself, without the creative work of Ariel, his 'industrious servant' (4.1.33) who is also a 'tricksy spirit' (5.1.227). Prospero, master and magician, who speaks at length in the play, but does not sing, is inextricably connected to his instruments, those spirits whose high voices indicate an apparent lack of masculine power. But with their own quasi-musical eloquence and agendas, these characters are often a disruptive presence in a world notionally under male control. This is as true for Emilia and Desdemona (signalling a different world of emotional understanding with the Willow Song) as it is for the fairy queens of *A Midsummer Night's Dream* and *The Merry Wives of Windsor*; for the distracted Ophelia as for the guilt-ridden Lady Macbeth – both of whom ultimately are not capable of 'masculine' rationality. The best opera composers instinctively understand this and embody it in their music.

One of the most interesting and thoughtful of English operas, Michael Tippett's *The Knot Garden* (1970), consciously evokes this scheme of contrasts (masculine/feminine, rational/dream-state, empowered/powerless). It involves a series of encounters between a mid-twentieth-century Prospero-like psychotherapist called Mangus, various female characters, and two gay male artists. Tippet gave the opera the title of the Renaissance emblem, the 'knot garden' – an enigmatic topographical construct that sits, like music, between the tangible and the ineffably mysterious. The knot-garden is thus a magical place, like Prospero's island. The opera begins with a 'storm' prelude, like that in *The Tempest* – a device for bringing all the characters together in one place. Some of Tippett's small cast of characters are modelled on Shakespearean prototypes: Mangus sees himself as Prospero; Faber is a version of Ferdinand; Flora, of Miranda; and Mel and Dov are Caliban and Ariel. In the opera's culminating act Mangus declares that his production of *The Tempest* has begun: 'This garden is now an island', and the characters play out the roles Mangus assigns them. When they are on the brink of resolving their problems, Tippett quotes his own setting of Ariel's song, 'Come unto these yellow sands' (written for an Old Vic Theatre production of *The Tempest* in 1961). Significantly, Faber's wife Thea and the political activist Denise – articulate modern women – do not take on Shakespearean roles, but comment on the action, critical of Mangus's controlling and voyeuristic role as impresario of the drama. These female voices represent, like Ariel, an alternative to a still-powerful cultural narrative, that of male domination as the social norm. One might hazard that there is unlikely ever to be a full-scale opera based on any of Shakespeare's history plays (though there is much stirring theatre and film music for the patriotic agendas of *King Henry V*), simply because, at a basic structural level, those plays are 'one-note' – that of masculine rhetorical authority.

In the women's song 'Orpheus, with his lute', in Act 3, Scene 1, of *King Henry VIII*, Shakespeare writes eloquently of music's power: 'In sweet music is such art' (3.1.12). The philosophy of music in the Renaissance acknowledged its dual aspects of the ineffable and the carefully crafted – its dependence as much on mathematical theories as on the variety of human emotions. When opera began to establish its claims for musical and dramatic centrality, its characters' most individual and unpredictable utterances were underpinned by the rules of harmony and composition, and, as I have suggested, by the conventions of specific periods in European cultural history. Composers of musical drama seem always to have intuited, in the words of Boito, that 'music is the most omnipotent of the arts, it has a logic of its own, more rapid, more free than the logic of spoken thought, and far more eloquent'. The Shakespeare works that explore the supernatural, the feminine, the irrational, the powerless, and the subversively comic, can be given, in opera, an extra dimension of extraordinary power.

6

Shakespeare and the Novel

Graham Holderness

What has Shakespeare, poet and playwright of the past, to do with a quintessentially modern form like the novel?

The novel today is the dominant form of fictional literature, far more popular and central to the culture than is the theatre. Easily defined – as a long story, normally in prose, deploying a range of narrative perspectives, describing fully-realized fictional characters in a specific social setting, and usually published in the form of a printed book – the apparent familiarity of the form disguises a hugely diverse and varied body of writing.

When I first studied the novel, it was believed that the form originated in the eighteenth century with the fiction of Daniel Defoe, Henry Fielding and Samuel Richardson, and was synonymous with literary realism. The novel emerged from the Age of Reason, was closely associated with journalism, satire and conduct literature, and marked a profound break with the supernatural, fantastic and romance narratives of the past. Its perfect embodiment was to be found in the work of Jane Austen, even today an immensely popular writer, and widely regarded as a defining practitioner of the novel form.

Historians and critics charting 'the rise of the novel' naturally compared the form to its cultural predecessors: the ancient epic, the long narrative poem, and, especially, the early modern drama. Via such comparisons the term 'Shakespearean' came into use as a way of defining the character and value of modern prose fiction. This was to some extent a value judgement ('Shakespearean' being the highest achievable accolade for any kind of writing), but it also attempted to account for distinctive parallels that could be detected between Shakespearean drama and the novel. Both originated in popular culture: the drama to entertain city theatrical audiences of the sixteenth century, and the novel the emerging metropolitan reading public in the eighteenth. But both were subsequently acknowledged by the academy as 'high cultural' forms that transcended their popular roots to scale the uppermost levels of artistic achievement.

The novel was, from the eighteenth century onwards, recognized and valued for its capacity to represent whole societies, historical or contemporary, in detailed, comprehensive, analytical descriptions, culminating in the great nineteenth-century social novels of Balzac, Tolstoy and Dickens. But centuries earlier Shakespeare had created, in his plays, extraordinarily exact and convincing imitations of actual societies, from ancient Rome to contemporary Venice. Great tragedies like *Macbeth* and *King Lear* are remarkable in the way they present whole societies in convulsion and transformation.

The novel is also acknowledged as the literary pioneer of psychological realism, whereby 'characters' were deepened and rounded to form fully-realized, recognizable human beings with vivid inner lives. But in this respect fiction was merely extending the creation of psychological interiority for which Shakespeare is justly famous. Prince Hamlet's soliloquies are acknowledged as landmarks in the artistic representation of a human being thinking, feeling, being, before our very eyes.

Many other parallels can be drawn between the novel and the Shakespearean drama. Unlike the English neo-Classical drama of the seventeenth and eighteenth centuries, both often feature multiple plots that mix social classes. Both employ what the literary theorist Mikhail Bakhtin called 'heteroglossia', the clash and interplay of different dramatic and narrative voices. Both effortlessly blend history, comedy, tragedy and romance; sentiment and irony; poetry and prose; reality and illusion, into extraordinarily complex but distinctively unified works of art. To call the novel 'Shakespearean' is not just to evaluate it by the gold standard of Shakespearean pre-eminence. It is also to draw attention to significant resonances between two historically discrepant, and chronologically discontinuous, cultural forms. These observations are predicated on the theory of the 'rise of the novel' in the eighteenth century. But we need to question this hypothesis in the light of the unfolding history of modern fiction. It is true that this restrictive view of the novel, invented by literary historians and critics, is still to be found in the reviewing practices of the quality press, and in the short-lists of prestigious literary prizes. But there is a huge gap between this highbrow conception of the novel, as a kind of ethically-informed social and psychological realism, and the actual practice and popularity of the form. A list of the best-selling novels of all time published in *The Guardian* was easily dominated by thrillers, magic, erotica and the Gothic: by Dan Brown, J. K. Rowling, E. L. James, and Stephenie Meyer. The novel encompasses both literary and popular fiction, and as such flourishes in myriad different genres: adventure, crime, romance, history, supernatural, Gothic, enchantment, utopian, dystopic, pornographic and so on. In addition, its form allows for the widest possible range of artistic experimentation, and for creative engagement with other media such as film, visual art, and digital technologies.

This diversity and flexibility of the novel form suggests that the notion of its history as coterminous with modernity is simply false, since long narratives of fantasy, romance and historical fiction go back some 2,000 years, and flourished in the Classical, medieval, and early-modern worlds. The term 'novel' derives from the Italian *novella*, a form of short story that was popular in the Renaissance, and that provided the plots for most of Shakespeare's comedies, and some of his tragedies. If the fictional prose narratives of Boccaccio, Bandello and Cinthio were 'novels', then the first link between Shakespeare and the novel is that many of his plays were initially derivative of the form. The novel is already inside Shakespeare, before we start to consider his subsequent impact on what we now know as the novel.

This reverses our traditional chronological assumptions about Shakespeare's influence over the novel, and suggests, rather, that Shakespeare not only stands as a landmark in a much longer history of fiction, but was himself a significant practitioner in the very modes of artistic representation – psychological and social realism, formal experiment and innovation, stylistic heterogeneity, heteroglossia – that the novel later came to demarcate as its own aesthetic territory. We might even say, paradoxically and with theoretical hindsight, that Shakespeare was himself a novelist. Shakespeare was able to incorporate plots, characters and themes from Italian novellas because the form of drama he practised was as diverse and varied as is our contemporary popular fiction, and his plays thrived not only on social, historical and psychological realism, but also on the imaginative plenitude and aesthetic flexibility of romance, adventure, enchantment, verbal extravagance, and metafiction.

The early practitioners of what we may call the 'modern novel' in the eighteenth century, basing their stories in the reality of contemporary life, could not adapt Shakespeare's works in the way that Shakespeare appropriated the Italian novel. This kind of novel was in every respect different from Shakespeare: it was new, 'novel', not old; it was prose, not poetry; it was narrative, not dramatic; it was realist, not magical; it was fictional, not metafictional. Hence in the novels of Fielding and Richardson Shakespeare is quoted, cited as a notable source of poetic wisdom, rather than adapted. In Richardson's epistolary novel *Clarissa* (1747–8) the hero Lovelace quotes from *Othello* – 'Perdition catch my soul, but I do love her!' – to illustrate the vehemence of his passion. In turn Clarissa castigates Lovelace's 'extravagant volubility' with another Shakespeare quotation (from *A Midsummer Night's Dream*), censuring him as an untrustworthy purveyor of 'saucy and audacious eloquence' (5.1.103). The characters interpolate Shakespeare quotations into their letters in much the same way as they would introduce such quotations into polite conversation: Clarissa expresses contempt for a woman who quotes Shakespeare 'with a theatrical air'. Shakespeare forms a staple of polite conversation: Jane Austen has her Henry Crawford say, in chapter thirty-four of *Mansfield Park* (1814), 'Shakespeare one gets acquainted with without knowing how. It is a part of an Englishman's constitution'. Shakespeare is brought into Richardson's novel as both an unruly poet of transgressive passion, and as the supreme representative of unreliable artifice, the dissimulation of the drama. Both are kept firmly at a distance, outside the text, by the rational mimesis and respectable morality of the novel's narrator.

Henry Fielding, by contrast, satirized the pretentiousness of quoting Shakespeare, both in the person of the narrator and through his characters. But, in keeping with other modern novelists, he also registered the presence of Shakespeare in the social world he depicted by describing theatres, actors, spectators and plays. In Book 16 of *Tom Jones* (1749), Partridge is taken to see *Hamlet*, and views the play innocently via 'the simple dictates of nature, unimproved, indeed, but likewise unadulterated, by art'. Thus on seeing the

Ghost, Partridge is initially sceptical that he is really viewing a spirit: though he's never seen a ghost, he's sure one wouldn't look like that. But he is then persuaded by the manifest terror of the actor – none other than Garrick himself – to 'credit' that the Ghost is, after all, real. Here the novel's style of mock-heroic realism draws a clear line between Shakespeare and reality, and satirizes the power of theatre to instil, through emotion, a belief in a manifest falsehood.

These novelists keep Shakespeare at a distance. The distinctive exception in eighteenth-century fiction is Laurence Sterne's *The Life and Opinions of Tristram Shandy, Gentleman* (1759–67), an experimental comic novel that has been regarded as a prototype of postmodern fiction. By contrast with Fielding and Richardson, Sterne invites Shakespeare inside his text, inventing the character of Parson Yorick, said to be descended from Yorick the king's jester, whose skull is exhumed in *Hamlet*. Here realism is inverted, and fact grounded in fiction. Yorick's death takes place early in the novel, and is memorialized by the epitaph 'Alas poor Yorick!', and by the metafictional interpolation into the text of a blank black page. In *Tristram Shandy* we see the boundaries of the novel being extended by stylistic experiment in such a way as to render possible the inclusion and incorporation of Shakespeare.

Yet at the same time, the dramatic text is not merely a rich source for proto-postmodern experiment, since virtually all the stylistic innovations Sterne introduces already have their counterparts in *Hamlet*. The graveyard scene, from which Yorick derives, displays abundantly that dislocating rapprochement of seriousness and humour, sincerity and playfulness, realism and metadrama that Sterne imitated from Shakespeare. The most profound religious and philosophical reflections on mortality jostle energetically with the most outrageous examples of black humour. The dramatic perspective and the medium of theatrical language is continually shifting, from prince to peasant, king to clown, past to present, just as the graveyard's occupants demonstrate the common fate of all humanity. The scene is at one moment medieval Denmark – 'he that is mad and sent into England' (*Hamlet*, 5.1.147) – and now the stage of the Globe theatre in 1601: "Twill not be seen in him there. There the men are as mad as he' (5.1.153–4). All the fantasy, humour, imagination, wit, verbal dexterity, playful artifice, and self-reflective fictionality that characterize Shakespearean drama found their natural home in the experimental novel.

The 'Age of Enlightenment' that produced the modern novel was soon revolutionized by the paradigm shift we know as Romanticism. Simultaneously, Shakespeare's own reputation was transformed from neo-Classical reserve to full-blown adulation. Poets and dramatists began to draw much more freely on his work, and the novelists followed suit. A key example is that of Sir Walter Scott, credited as the father of the modern historical novel. He recognized Shakespeare as a great historical and social chronicler, and extended that admiration into formal imitation. In his *Ivanhoe* (1820) Shakespeare furnishes Scott with his portrait of the Middle Ages. Shakespeare was considered part of the furniture of the educated mind, so Scott could assume his readers would recognize his allusions. His Prince John resembles Shakespeare's King John, his Wamba, the Fool in *King Lear*, his Richard I, Shakespeare's Henry V. Above all, Scott drew on *The Merchant of Venice* for his depiction of the Jewish merchant and moneylender Isaac of York, signalling the parallel by epigraphical Shakespeare quotations, and extrapolating the sympathetic and humane elements of Shakespeare's treatment of Shylock, especially in the portrayal of Isaac's daughter Rebecca, in order to undertake a challenging revision of what he saw as Elizabethan prejudice against Jews. In this respect Scott may have been indebted to Maria Edgeworth, who drew on *The Merchant of Venice* extensively for the structure of her pro-Jewish novel *Harrington* (1817). Written in response to a letter from a Jewish-American reader who complained about Edgeworth's anti-semitic portrayals of Jews in her earlier novels, *Harrington* tells the story of a man whose anti-semitic prejudices are undermined by his association with various Jewish characters. To some degree in *Ivanhoe* Scott was using Shakespeare as a portal to the past, paradoxically reconstructing a historical Middle Ages out of partly fictional rather than factual materials.

Running alongside the realist social and historical novels of Scott and Jane Austen was the very different tradition of the Gothic novel, which naturally found inspiration in Shakespeare's supernatural materials, especially the Ghost in *Hamlet* and *Macbeth*'s witches. The two streams coalesced in the fiction of the Brontë sisters. Emily Brontë's *Wuthering Heights* (1847) explicitly alludes to *King Lear*, and structures its action very much like a revenge tragedy. Heathcliff resembles some of Shakespeare's most monstrous villains, Iago or Richard III; Cathy's delusions echo Ophelia's. Here the modern novelist goes to Shakespeare not for social realism or historical colour, but for portraits of vindictive passion, grotesque monstrosity, visionary madness. Shakespeare and the novel converge on the grounds of psychological extremity, supernatural vision, and imaginative insanity.

Charlotte Brontë, less resolutely Gothic than her sister, nonetheless found a place for Shakespeare – see the chapter entitled 'Coriolanus' in *Shirley* (1849), her 'social problem' novel on industrial conflicts. The 'democrat' Caroline Helston insists that the reactionary mill-owner Robert Moore should read Shakespeare, not for moral instruction, but to internalize his poetic wisdom, 'to take some of his soul into yours'. They read *Coriolanus* together, and Caroline prompts Robert to find in himself the patrician pride that blocks sympathy for his employees, just as Coriolanus is unable to sympathize with his 'famished fellow-men'. The lesson does not take, and Moore is drawn rather to the Roman's 'irrational pride'. Nonetheless his reading of Shakespeare proves to be the beginning of an education in humane sympathy: 'As he advanced, he forgot to criticise; it was evident he appreciated the power, the truth of each portion; and, stepping out of the narrow line of private prejudices, began to revel in the large picture of human nature, to feel the reality stamped upon the characters who were speaking from that page before him'. The importance of this example is that Charlotte Brontë incorporated into her novel not only a reference to Shakespeare, but a serious critical debate about the ultimate meaning of one of his plays. Shakespearean fiction and its horizons of interpretation lie close to hand among the sources of the novel's social realism.

The greatest of the nineteenth-century novelists, Charles Dickens, was a lover of the theatre, and a life-long Shakespeare enthusiast. At times he carried a volume of Shakespeare in his pocket, and he bought a house mainly for its associations with Gad's Hill, the scene of Falstaff's robbery in *King Henry IV*, Part 1. He was an active member of the Shakespeare Society, and of the London Shakespeare Committee, which bought Shakespeare's Birthplace. He even acted in performances of Shakespeare plays. All of Dickens's novels contain allusions to Shakespeare; and Shakespeare plays are performed, always in comic contexts, in his novels from the beginning to the end of his career, from *Othello* in *Sketches by Boz* (1837–9) to *Hamlet* in *Great Expectations* (1860–1). In *Nicholas Nickleby* (1838–9) the hero joins a travelling theatre company, and, in chapter twenty-five, plays Romeo. Dickens's wider interest in Shakespeare scholarship is reflected when, in the same novel, he satirizes a scholar who 'proved that by altering the received pronunciation, any of Shakespeare's plays could be made to mean quite different'.

And yet Dickens's uses of Shakespeare tend to resemble those of the eighteenth-century novelists, in that Shakespeare is an element of the culture and society he was representing, rather than a source to be adapted or appropriated. There are a few exceptions to this in his earlier work: for instance the spectre of *King Lear* hovers round the relationship between the old father and his virtuous Cordelia-like daughter in *The Old Curiosity Shop* (1840–1). But in general, although Dickens made extensive use of romance plots and of fantasy, he wanted his fiction to be read as rooted in real life, even when it touches extreme improbability, such as a man in *Bleak House* (1852–3) dying of internal combustion. To ground a novel explicitly in Shakespearean fiction was not part of his novelistic method. A useful contrast is provided by Oscar Wilde's novel *The Picture of Dorian Gray* (1890), which also features a theatre, actors, and a Shakespeare play. Dorian falls in love with a young actress, Sibyl Vane, on seeing her play Shakespearean heroines such as Juliet. But here Shakespeare is far more than an objective social reality to be represented. The artifice, beauty, and passion of Shakespearean drama here represent art, a reality higher than that of actual human life. Once Sibyl reveals herself, in chapter seven, to be a fallible human being, indeed a very poor actress, Dorian is immediately disenchanted. Only when she emulates Shakespeare in her suicide does he again find her interesting and moving. Reality and fantasy have changed places, and Shakespeare is re-positioned as a cornerstone of the true reality to be found in art.

Wilde's aestheticism prefigured the next cultural movement to shift the paradigm of novelistic Shakespeare, modernism. In the early twentieth century the novel was transformed in the hands of writers who broke with the dominant traditions of nineteenth-century fiction, disrupting the sequential cause-and-effect of traditional narrative, fracturing the unity of plot and coherence of character, using ironic and ambiguous juxtapositions to challenge literary meaning, and foregrounding inward consciousness over rational, objective discourse. Social reality became distorted through the lens of the individual character's 'stream-of-consciousness'; language became a dense, complex substance containing rather than reflecting reality and meaning; and the novel itself was reconceived as a relatively autonomous artefact, and a space of aesthetic experiment. In this environment novelists were able to incorporate Shakespeare into the novel in new, exciting and very influential ways.

Virginia Woolf often cited Shakespeare in her writings. In her essay *A Room of One's Own* (1929) she invented an imaginary 'Shakespeare's sister', 'Judith', who, as a woman, despite her talent, was unable to equal her brother. The hero/heroine of her novel *Orlando* (1928) draws on the androgyny of Shakespeare's comedies, and the work also features a brief cameo appearance, in chapter two, by Shakespeare himself. And Shakespeare features strikingly in Woolf's last novel, *Between the Acts* (1941). Set in 'traditional' country-house and rural-village England, about to be overwhelmed by war, the central action of the novel entails the performance of a historical pageant before an audience of the main characters. Shakespearean romance supplies the first of these, the others being a spoof Restoration drama and a Victorian melodrama. But the presence of Shakespeare also pervades the novel, in the form of quotations and misquotations supplied by both the characters and the narrator. Many of these come from *Troilus and Cressida*, Shakespeare's bitter play about the Trojan War, which supplies a parallel for Britain on the brink of the Second World War. The pervasive presence of Shakespeare in the texture of the novel indicates the extent to which his writing forms part of the material of British culture, and the substructure of the characters' minds. Thus when the pageant closes by holding mirrors up to the audience, confronting the spectators with a direct reflection of contemporary life, Shakespeare is both the mirror, and an element of what is being reflected in it. The experimental form of the modernist novel has allowed Shakespeare to enter the charmed circle of the artefact, not as a social reality to be displayed, but as part of the very fabric of social existence that the novel form seeks to emulate.

Similarly, in what is arguably the greatest modernist novel, James Joyce's *Ulysses* (1922), Shakespeare again becomes part of the fabric of the work. As in Woolf, this initially takes the form of a specific manifestation of Shakespeare within the novel's social milieu: in Chapter 9, Joyce's hero, Stephen Dedalus, is arguing about Shakespeare's life with a group of intellectuals in the National Library in Dublin. Stephen argues that the emotions dramatized in Shakespeare's *Hamlet* can be traced to the poet's own personal experience of bereavement (of son and father), and an alleged betrayal by his conjecturally adulterous wife. But in these pages Joyce is also devising, within the medium of fiction, a method for talking about the relations between a writer and his writing. Speaking of *Hamlet*, Joyce writes: 'Through the ghost of the unquiet father the image of the unliving son looks forth.' As he played the role of the Ghost on stage, Shakespeare was both son and father, conveying through his own poetry the grief of the bereaved son, and speaking as a father to the prince who was his own son's namesake. This metafictional dimension of the novel, which both invites awareness of its own artifice and internalizes literary-critical debate and interpretation, opens up to us the porousness of the novel form, and makes us aware of the shifting borderlines between individuals and personalities both inside and outside fiction.

The Shakespearean experiments of Woolf and Joyce made it possible for later modernist writers to draw Shakespeare ever deeper and closer into the structure, texture, and fabric of the novel. In part one of Iris Murdoch's *The Black Prince* (1973), a complex and deeply philosophical story about love and art, Shakespeare is initiated into the narrative quite unobtrusively by the plot device of a schoolgirl, Julian, asking her middle-aged family friend Arnold Baffin for advice about *Hamlet* for her homework. The conversation about Shakespeare expands and intensifies along with Arnold's obsessive passion for Julian. The two are brought together on the ground of this Shakespearean conversation, and Arnold discovers the sexual arousal he has lacked only when Julian dresses herself in theatrical costume as Prince Hamlet, with a sheep's skull. The 'black prince' of the title is both Hamlet and a Platonic 'dark god' of transgressive desire. The brief temporary passion between the elderly writer and the young girl seems (at least to Arnold himself, who is narrating at this point) to bring love and art together. Murdoch infiltrates Shakespearean language directly into character as well as plot, allowing Arnold to speak and even think in lines from several Shakespeare plays, and especially his *Sonnets*. Frequently, lines of Shakespeare lie ambiguously on the page, leaving the reader uncertain as to their status as quotation, recorded speech, thought or narrative. The discrepant idioms of Shakespeare and the novel have at last found a common ground.

A novelist whose work has been claimed for both modernism and postmodernism, Antony Burgess, exerted a potent influence on the next stage of development for Shakespeare and the novel. Burgess thought of himself as a polymathic artist, writing novels, poetry, music, drama, film and TV screenplays, and literary criticism. His long-term relationship with Shakespeare produced critical articles and reviews, a ballet suite, a TV series, a musical, the critical biography *Shakespeare* (1970), and a novel on Shakespeare's life, *Nothing Like the Sun* (1964). The two latter texts have much in common, since in the biography Burgess used scholarship imaginatively and creatively, while the novel is permeated by biographical and critical questions about writing and writers, the past and the present, the relations between literature and life.

The story of *Nothing Like the Sun* draws on the more speculative side of Shakespeare biography: Shakespeare has a full-blown affair with the Earl of Southampton and is infected with syphilis by a black prostitute, the 'Dark Lady'. Formally it is a historical novel, though much more modernist than most historical fiction of the time. The style of the novel combines an idiom of invented Elizabethan rhetoric, permeated by Shakespeare quotation, with the experimental liberty and self-reflexive playfulness of modernist prose, so the reader is continually aware that a reconstructed past, fashioned from largely fictional materials, is being transmuted through a modern sensibility. Burgess's Shakespeare often thinks in the language of his own plays, and other characters frequently provide him with some of his most familiar lines, simultaneously inventing and quoting them in advance. Passages from the plays are deployed to evidence the events of Shakespeare's life, love, betrayal, disease. In one sense Burgess's literary biography and his novel mirror one another, since in his *Shakespeare* the life illustrates the plays, while in *Nothing Like the Sun* the plays illuminate the life. In its synthesis of scholarship and imagination, its metafictional playing with past and present, its mixing of genres and collocation of styles, *Nothing Like the Sun* pushed the Shakespeare novel into the new territory of postmodernism.

Nothing Like the Sun is a novel of Shakespeare's life, rather than one based on his works, and thus belongs to a prolific and popular sub-genre recently revitalized by the success of the 1998 film *Shakespeare in Love*. From the 1970s onwards, however, it became possible for novelists to appropriate Shakespeare's works directly, and with a freedom and privilege previously unknown to the modern novel. Novels could be unashamedly based in fiction rather than in fact. Writers could assume, on the part of their readers, at least a minimal knowledge of Shakespeare, and could build plots, and fashion characters, explicitly from Shakespearean sources. In addition, with the massive expansion of higher education, and the turn towards literary and cultural theory in the humanities, novelists could presuppose, alongside a knowledge of Shakespeare, a readerly interest in questions of cultural politics and problems of class, race, and gender. On this basis some novelists have approached Shakespeare oppositionally, conceiving of him as (in the critic Kathleen McLuskie's phrase) the 'patriarchal bard', or as the embodiment of colonial power, or as the custodian of repressive morality. Such novelists have explicitly adapted his plays and characters to service projects in the reassessment of gender, race, and sexuality. Novels such as Robert Nye's *Falstaff* (1976), Erica Jong's *Shylock's Daughter* (originally titled *Serenissima* [1987]), Angela Carter's *Wise Children* (1991), Jane Smiley's *A Thousand Acres* (1991), Marina Warner's *Indigo* (1992), Caryl Phillips's *The Nature of Blood* (1997), and John Updike's *Gertrude and Claudius* (2000) all belong to this movement.

In our own twenty-first century the Shakespearean novel is undergoing a Renaissance. The long prose narrative has been energized by interfaces with different media, especially TV, film and the Internet. New methods of publishing and consuming literature have transformed the nature of readership into an interactive participation. The postmodern collapsing of generic restrictions has enabled Shakespeare to migrate much more comprehensively across previously sealed boundaries, into popular genres such as crime fiction, paranormal romance, dystopian fable, and supernatural fantasy. In contemporary fiction Shakespeare himself is as likely to be found killing zombies or vampires as writing poems and plays. Major fiction writers have based whole novels on Shakespeare plays. *101 Reykjavik* (1996, trans. 2002), by the Icelander Hallgrímur Helgason, *Something Rotten* (2004) by the British author Jasper Fforde, and *Lunar Park* (2005), by the American Brett Easton Ellis, are all direct and explicit re-workings of *Hamlet*. In a landmark publishing initiative, the Hogarth Press is making available new novels inspired by Shakespeare's works, including Anne Tyler on *The Taming of the Shrew*; Jeanette Winterson on *The Winter's Tale*; Margaret Atwood on *The Tempest*; Howard Jacobson on *The Merchant of Venice*; Tracy Chevalier on *Othello*; Gillian Flynn on *Hamlet*; and the Swedish thriller writer Jo Nesbo will undertake a version of *Macbeth*. This powerful and cosmopolitan team of authors, whose work encompasses a wide range of fictional styles, will confirm and endorse the status of the Shakespearean novel as a global phenomenon for the twenty-first century.

This chapter has in effect traced, chronologically, the spine of a huge, diverse, and continually evolving organism we know as the Shakespearean novel, making no attempt to comprehend its massive and prolifically expanding body. My chronological survey has concentrated on major authors of British fiction. Many other authors, including Shakespeare scholars, have written Shakespearean novels. And the Shakespearean novel is by no means a solely British product: a fuller account would have to bestow more attention at least on novels from North America, the former British colonies, and the Middle East. But it should be possible to apprehend, on the basis of this very selective corpus of texts by indisputably important authors, the historical evolution of the Shakespearean novel. Fiction writers now can imitate and adapt Shakespeare's plays as easily as he was able to adapt the novel into drama. Over four centuries, Shakespeare's plays have undergone some remarkable transformations, but none so striking as the gradual evolution of the novel form to a point where Shakespeare, poet and playwright of yesterday, could be so readily and successfully incorporated into the fiction of today.

7

Shakespeare and Film and Television

Russell Jackson

In the earliest years of the cinema, Shakespearean performance took its place among news items for short programmes in music halls – surviving examples are Herbert Beerbohm Tree dying as King John (GB, 1899) and Sarah Bernhardt fencing as Hamlet (France, 1900). The plays soon became a source for more extended 'photoplays'. These ranged from episodes from theatre performances, such as the Benson company in *Richard III* (GB, 1911), to carefully crafted dramas featuring eminent actors, such as the *Hamlet* films, with Sir Johnston Forbes-Robertson (GB, 1913) and Ruggero Ruggeri (Italy, 1917). By the 1920s audiences could expect complex storytelling. Although the gestural codes of actors still retained some of the broadness associated with the melodramatic stage, it was possible for *Hamlet. Drama of Revenge* (Germany, 1920) to offer both finesse in the playing of the popular star Asta Neilsen as Hamlet (a woman disguised for reasons of state as a man) and exaggeration in the Claudius of Eduard von Winterstein, the most patently villainous Danish usurper ever committed to celluloid. As in the 1922 *Othello* filmed in Germany with Emil Jannings and Werner Krauss, acting of this order seems puzzling in view of the natural-seeming underplaying achieved in other roles by the same actors.

The advent of synchronized sound imposed new responsibilities that made the plays less amenable to adaptation and international distribution. The estimated number of silent versions of the plays – between 250 and 300, most of them no longer extant – outstrips the tally from the first decades of the sound era. Between 1927 and 1950 only seven full-length feature films of the plays were released: *The Taming of the Shrew* (USA, 1929), *A Midsummer Night's Dream* (USA, 1935), *Romeo and Juliet* (USA, 1936), *As You Like It* (GB, 1936), *Henry V* (GB, 1944), *Hamlet* (GB, 1948) and *Macbeth* (USA, 1949).

The first of these, *The Taming of the Shrew*, with Mary Pickford and Douglas Fairbanks, has elements that would be needed to make the studios – and, they hoped, their public – pay for Shakespeare. There had to be stars – and here Katherina and Petruchio were played by two of the biggest stars in Hollywood, together on screen for the first time. The production values must be the best the studio could achieve and prestige might compensate for lack of box-office profit. And the studio had to be able to claim 'authenticity' for the film, in respect of the text and in the recreation of the setting. Lavish realizations of city streets, *palazzi*, and forests characterize the Shakespeare films of the 1930s: MGM's *Romeo and Juliet* (with Leslie Howard and Norma Shearer as the somewhat-too-mature lovers); *As You like It* with the Austrian star Elisabeth Bergner as Rosalind opposite Laurence Olivier as Orlando; and *A Midsummer Night's Dream*. For the last of these Max Reinhardt and William Dieterle marshaled extraordinary forces: an accomplished cast that included James Cagney as Bottom; choreography by Bronislava Nijinska; Erich Wolfgang Korngold's score arranged from Mendelssohn; and a forest set that covered two sound stages. Although none of these films were wholly successful in financial terms, and some of the casting and other decisions may have misfired, they do reflect the desire of directors and actors to extend the range of the medium and satisfy their own artistic ambitions. John Barrymore is an eccentric but dynamic Mercutio, Olivier's Orlando is ardent and lyrical, and Cagney is a fine Bottom, bringing charm and vulnerability to the role. The Reinhardt and Dieterle film represents a great theatre director's cumulative experience of a play he had staged many times since 1905. Whatever the studio's commercial motives – prestige was a more likely outcome than financial profit – the Shakespeare films of the 1930s represent a laudable wish to extend the range of 'raw material' the movies could draw on. Shakespeare was a challenge filmmakers hoped to rise to.

These productions were promoted as historical costume dramas, to be judged alongside others from the major studios. That Laurence Olivier was able, despite wartime conditions, to make his *Henry V* a contender in the same category was attributable to the resources allotted to a patriotic (but not vainglorious) subject, one that responded to the audience's appetite in a dark time for colourful and engaging spectacle, and had the bonus of cultural respectability. Like *Henry V*, Olivier's 1948 *Hamlet*, in black-and-white, drew on a roster of Shakespearean actors from the British stage. The cuts and adjustments in *Hamlet*, including the omission of Rosencrantz and Guildenstern and the Fortinbras dimension of the plot, were no obstacle to the perception of this as 'authentic' Shakespeare. The effect was enhanced by the clarity and 'Englishness' of speech, in the received pronunciation of the time, familiar on stage and radio.

A challenge to this definition of authenticity, and to the values of the 'well-made film', came with Orson Welles's *Macbeth* (1949) and his subsequent *Othello* (1952). Both were made under unusual conditions: the first largely by choice, the second as a result of financial constraint. *Macbeth* originated in Welles's 1936 stage production – the 'Voodoo' *Macbeth* – and takes place in a cruel, pre-Christian Scotland of the imagination, with sets that suggest a series of damp caves. Although Welles made the mistake of having the cast perform in would-be authentic Scottish accents – and had to redub as well as recut after early screenings – he was more successful in his quest for authenticity of another kind, exploring the play as a tragic myth, with the hero's anguish at the forefront. Welles looms large, in every sense, in all the films he directed, and here his character's intervention in the queen's sleepwalking scene seems like an example of his egocentricity. Where Olivier's *Hamlet* was claimed in his introductory voice-over as the tragedy of a man who could not make up his mind, Welles's *Macbeth* became the tragedy of one who made it up all too decisively, with the wrong kind of 'metaphysical aid' (1.5.28). For all its shortcomings, this *Macbeth* is weirdly compulsive while Olivier's *Hamlet* is languorously elegiac.

Welles's *Othello* is a film of contrasts, set in a world where moral, emotional, and physical darkness are in conflict with light from the very first images on the screen, as the dead Othello's face emerges from blackness, inverted as he lies on his bier. Although a series of financial crises caused the film to be shot in locations across two continents, with Welles re-voicing some characters in post-production, there is an intelligible sense of a world where life continues in contrast to the emotional turmoil created in its central characters. Shadows, canted camera angles, ominously plangent music, and (at times) abnormally resonant speech continue the expressionism of *Macbeth*. Like his later *Chimes at Midnight* (1964), a Falstaff-centred saga derived mainly from the two parts of *King Henry IV*, Welles's *Othello* shares with his other completed Shakespearean projects a passionate commitment to stories that command attention in every frame.

It is difficult to separate these films from the alarums and excursions of Welles's artistic career, a story framed by the director himself as an epic struggle against the film industry's 'system'. Back in the system's home, one notable Shakespeare film was achieved during this period: *Julius Caesar*, directed by Joseph L. Mankiewicz for MGM (1953). This was given plain but handsome Classical settings and filmed in black-and-white to evoke newsreel footage of the European totalitarian regimes, rather than a conventionally glamorized 'Ancient Rome'. Marlon Brando plays Mark Antony, alongside two British actors with firmly established Shakespearean credentials, John Gielgud (Cassius) and James Mason (Brutus). Brando's eloquent performance, especially in the Forum scene, gave the lie to critics who anticipated a reproduction of the vocal and physical mannerisms of his Stanley Kowalski in *A Streetcar Named Desire* (1951).

Drama productions in the new rival medium of television had begun on both sides of the Atlantic before the Second World War and returned, with television itself, after the cessation of hostilities. The small screen, low picture resolution, limited scenic resources, and confined broadcast time slots, meant that there was no chance of confusing a television version of a Shakespearean drama with one made on film for the cinema. On the other hand, in the early years there was the appeal of a sense of occasion in what was usually a one-off performance before the cameras. Directors in Britain and the United States found ways of making a distinctively televisual form of dramatic performance, achieving a flow from one set to another on the studio floor that evoked a sense of space beyond what was visible on screen. Although limited in number, American television productions of the 1940s and 1950s showed an intriguing range of inventive approaches, from the modern dress *Julius Caesar*

(1949) and *Coriolanus* (1951) broadcast by CBS, to Peter Brook's radically adapted and adventurously staged *King Lear*, starring Orson Welles (1953), to Maurice Evans's *Hamlet* (CBS, 1953), based on his 'GI' theatre version, and the same actor's *commedia*-style *Taming of the Shrew* (NBC, 1956), which stages the wooing scene in a boxing ring.

By the 1960s and early 1970s the increased range of television drama was made clear by two remarkable BBC series based on the history plays. In *An Age of Kings* (1960) the plays from *King Henry VI, Part 1* to *King Henry V* were organized into a coherent narrative in fifteen episodes, each running for approximately one hour, recorded in the studio using a set whose architectural elements were appropriately decorated and modified for each episode. *The Wars of the Roses* (1964) presented the Royal Shakespeare Company's cycle of three plays, based on the three parts of *King Henry VI* and *Richard III*, a vision of this period in English history much darker than that of *An Age of Kings*, and which depicted the political system of the era as a machine of treachery and ambition. Both series benefitted from fine acting, but the RSC's cast, including Peggy Ashcroft as Margaret of Anjou, David Warner as Henry VI, and Ian Holm as Richard of Gloucester, had the advantage of a run in the theatre that was already acclaimed as a landmark in the company's history.

On the United States networks, 'live' studio-taped drama had already given way to series produced on film, and although Hallmark Hall of Fame continued to include Shakespearean performances among its weekly drama offerings, British productions soon dominated the market. Nevertheless, North American productions of note included Joseph Papp's lively *Much Ado About Nothing*, based on his successful New York Shakespeare Festival staging (broadcast in 1973), and a documentary, *Kiss Me, Petruchio* (1981) featuring Papp's Central Park production with Raul Julia and Meryl Streep.

Beyond the series devoted to Shakespeare, productions of the plays were included on British television in other streams of programming, such as 'Play of the Month' and 'Armchair Theatre'. The British commercial station ITV televised two RSC productions from 1976: *Macbeth*, with Judi Dench and Ian McKellen in a replication of the intimate staging at Stratford's Other Place, and a musical version of *The Comedy of Errors*, with Dench, Roger

Rees and Michael Williams. The former recreated the tense intimacy of the original studio production, while the latter, by its inclusion of the audience's responses to a 'main house' Stratford performance, enhanced the television viewers' sense of sharing in the verve and stylishness of the show. These were outstanding achievements, suggesting new approaches to both 'studio' and 'live' Shakespeare, but when the BBC, in conjunction with Time-Life, launched its series of the 'Complete Works' in 1978, the initial productions of the marathon were for the most part stolid and dutiful. After changes in the production team the series improved, and included some effective and adventurous work. Notable were Jane Howell's sequence of the *King Henry VI* plays and *Richard II*; the same director's *Titus Andronicus*; an *All's Well that Ends Well* with interiors derived from Dutch seventeenth-century paintings (directed by Elijah Moshinsky); and Jonathan Miller's *The Taming of the Shrew*. The series also featured some impressive individual performances, such as Alan Howard's Coriolanus and Derek Jacobi's Hamlet.

Because of its implicit claims to be definitive – a word avoided by most actors and directors – the series threatened (unlike *An Age of Kings*) to stand in the way of other television productions that might have been planned. In the event, this was not the case. The BBC, after all, was not the only player in town, and it was Granada Television, based in Manchester, that produced *King Lear* with Laurence Olivier (1982). Some of the most effective and intriguing versions were radical adaptations rather than 'faithful' productions in the spirit of the BBC/Time-Life series. In 1992 the BBC broadcast *Shakespeare: the Animated Tales*, a series of twelve condensed versions aimed at children and voiced by eminent actors. *Macbeth on the Estate* (1997) reworked the play in terms of drug use and gang warfare, and, in 2005, *Shakespeare Re-Told* adapted four plays in terms of modern situations and themes, including a *Macbeth* set in a Glaswegian restaurant. In 2012 the BBC launched a sequence of history plays, *The Hollow Crown*, comprising *Richard II*, the two parts of *King Henry IV*, as well as *King Henry V*. (A second series, *The Hollow Crown: The Wars of the Roses*, followed in 2016.) These were more thoroughly adapted than their equivalents from the 1960s and 1980s, perhaps with an eye to the competition from such series on historical subjects as *Rome* (2005–7) and *The Tudors* (2007–10).

Some cinema productions of the 1950s, 1960s and early 1970s had anticipated the shift in emphasis towards television by being shown in cinemas in Great Britain and on television in the USA. Notable examples were Olivier's *Richard III* (1955) and Peter Hall's *A Midsummer Night's Dream* (1968), derived from his 1959 Stratford production and its 1962 revival. Nevertheless, Shakespeare continued to feature occasionally in the mainstream cinema too. Progress seemed to go in fits and starts, with commercially successful movies inspiring confidence for a while among potential financiers. Franco Zeffirelli's lavish and rumbustious *The Taming of the Shrew* (1967) owed its appeal – and much of its finance – to its stars, Elizabeth Taylor and Richard Burton, and profited from media fascination with their very public private lives. His *Romeo and Juliet* (1968) is unashamedly romantic, with picturesque Italian locations as well as some studio scenes, and a pair of lovers played by relative unknowns – Leonard Whiting and Olivia Hussey. It can thus claim authenticity on two levels: the age of the protagonists and the Italian setting. Hailed as a 'youth' movie in tune with the spirit of the 1960s, Zeffirelli's film responded to an agenda for representations of teenagers in love that had changed radically since the 1950s, and had been set for this play on stage (1957) and film (1961) by the musical *West Side Story*. In one important respect, sexuality was now acceptable – indeed, required – as an element of the Veronese love affair. In Zeffirelli's film, as in Baz Lurhmann's exciting (or, to hostile viewers, frenetic) 1996 version, there is no depiction of sexual activity beyond kissing, but the lovers do share a bed. Zeffirelli's Juliet is seen naked to the waist, while Romeo displays a graceful back view to the camera. The unaffected and moving performances of Whiting and Hussey were complemented by John McEnery's caustic Mercutio, his sexual language made explicit by gesture as well as vocal delivery.

This change in standards is also reflected in Roman Polanski's *Macbeth* (1971), where the sexual relationship of the upwardly mobile young Macbeths (Jon Finch and Francesca Annis) is made clear, and Lady Macbeth is naked during her sleepwalking scene. More important in this case was the shocking realism of the film's violence, introduced early on with the brutal killing of a wounded soldier on the battlefield, and the creation of a convincingly 'real' society. Unlike the caverns measureless to man inhabited by Welles's

Macbeth, these are castles in which normal feudal life continues, but which are nonetheless susceptible to the horrible imaginings of the director as well as those of the protagonist. In this respect Polanski's *Macbeth* has echoes of his *Repulsion* (1965) and *Rosemary's Baby* (1968). The cruelty is comparable to that in Peter Brook's *King Lear* (1971), set in a primitive kingdom where mere survival is an ordeal. Brook shows Gloucester's blinding and the suicide of Goneril with shock effects produced by editing and disorientation of the spectator's vision as much as by the realism of the physical acts themselves. Black-and-white cinematography enhances the bleakness of the film, although to very different effect from that of the epic *King Lear* (1969) by the Russian director Grigori Kozintsev. Brook's Lear (Paul Scofield), monumental and impregnable in his silence when first seen, becomes a figure of pitiful, deluded incapacity in the final sequence as he falls out of the frame to die. His first word, 'Know', sounds very like 'no', and his death delivers him to nothingness. Kozintsev shows a frail king (Yuri Yarvets) whose throne is supported by outmoded political assumptions whose inefficacy he does not perceive until it is too late. Brook ends with a Beckettian sense of the absurd. Kozintsev's final shot suggests the possibility of reconstruction after a civil war. For the Russian, meaning exists: here, as in his remarkable *Hamlet* (1964), it subsists in the material, political world and must be challenged and reassessed.

The Japanese director Akira Kurosawa may be said to offer a halfway point between these two approaches. His 1957 *Macbeth* film, known in English-speaking countries as *Throne of Blood*, frames the career of its protagonist with the reminder, in image and off-screen song, of the transitory and delusory nature of human ambition and achievement, while the code of allegiance that he breaks is devoid of the element of sanctity present in Duncan's kingship. Washizu dies in a hail of arrows shot by his own men from within his castle walls, a fate that has been predicted by supernatural forces but which is entirely attributable to mundane factors. The film's use of performance conventions from Japanese theatre results in a powerful and, at times, disorienting combination of realism and stylization, in which the viewer shares a degree of Washizu's bewilderment. In *Ran* (1987), Kurosawa's variation on the *King Lear* story, the ageing lord has been a cruel tyrant, and the chaos (the meaning of the title) initiated when he divides his responsibilities between his three sons is both pathetic and, in the last analysis, fully merited. Here, as in other films from cultures beyond those of Hollywood and Europe, Shakespeare's central narratives appear to Western audiences in a new and revitalizing context. In Vishal Bhardwaj's *Omkara* (India, 2006), *Othello* becomes a story of rival gangs and politicians, with the production values and appeal of Bollywood, and Xiaogang Feng's *The Banquet* (China, 2006) uses *Hamlet* in a spectacle of martial arts, historical spectacle (largely invented), and dynastic shenanigans.

Such Shakespeare-inspired movies from beyond the Anglophone film industry take what they find most useful from their source material. It could be claimed that all productions in any medium do so, even when they aspire to deliver the 'originals', but a distinctive tradition of adaptations can be traced, in which a play's stories and characters serve as an armature on which a new work has been fashioned. In some, the original is followed closely, even to the extent of incorporating to varied effect scenes and (sometimes word-for-word) speeches. *Joe Macbeth* (1954) and *Men of Respect* (1991) are mafia versions of the same tragedy, while Edgar Ulmer's weirdly expressionistic thriller *Strange Illusion* (1945), and Ingmar Bergman's family saga *Fanny and Alexander* (1982), have the psychological and sexual tensions of *Hamlet* in common. In some cases, such as in the Falstaff and Hal storyline in Gus Van Sant's *My Own Private Idaho* (1991), the 'fit' between Shakespeare and a contemporary narrative is perfect. In others, such as Tom Blake Nelson's *O* (2002), which transposes *Othello* into a context of contemporary racial politics and college basketball, the outcome is less secure. At the same time, the film addresses important racial and sexual stereotypes through its representation of a closed society – the elite school – to which the hero is admitted on sufferance because of his prowess on the basketball court. Something similar seems to happen with Oliver Parker's conventional *Othello* (1995), though neither is as problematic as Stuart Burge's 1965 film of the National Theatre's stage production, in which Olivier's Moor, famously powerful on stage, comes across as a caricature, his carefully crafted body language and vocal delivery seeming to many critics to approach a parody of black behaviour. This is doubly unfortunate, because at many moments Olivier is convincingly the authoritative, physically powerful, and tender Moor that few other actors have been able to deliver. Although many of the other performances are impressive – especially Frank Finlay's matter-of-fact Iago and the Desdemona of Maggie Smith – the film is hampered by the decision to shoot an only slightly adapted version of the theatre production on a film studio sound-stage, using an opened-out version of the original design.

In Michael Almereyda's *Hamlet* (2000), with Ethan Hawke, the dialogue is that of the play, but the film is on the demarcation line (if one is needed) between delivering the play with some degree of 'faithfulness' and the more freewheeling adaptations that also situate the story in a corporate milieu. In *The Rest is Silence* (Germany, 1959), young 'John Claudius' returns from the United States to confront unspoken truths about the wartime origins of his family's prosperity in West Germany's postwar 'Economic Miracle'. Kurosawa's *The Bad Sleep Well* (Japan, 1960) similarly draws on themes of guilt and recrimination in a period of national reconstruction. With less political resonance, the hero of the bizarre *Hamlet Goes Business* (Finland, 1987) confronts a villainous stepfather who is asset-stripping the family timber business, turning it over to the production of plastic ducks. It seems that structures of power and exploitation in commerce (or its less respectable cousin, the Mafia) make for a more effective analogy than their equivalents in modern politics for the court of Shakespeare's Elsinore. Here the expectations of a popular film genre are also at work.

'Tragedy' does not figure as a recognized film genre, at least as represented on the labeling used by studios and distributors. 'Fantasy', of course, does. Currently prevailing examples of the cinema of fantasy set standards for *A Midsummer Night's Dream*, which have been met with varying success by Reinhardt and Dieterle in 1935 and Michael Hoffmann in 1999. In a similar vein, the films of *The Tempest* by Derek Jarman (1980) and Julie Taymor (2011) offer not only contrasting interpretations of the play but also opposing definitions of this kind of film-making: Jarman's, set in a crumbling mansion, achieves the home-made (or artisanal) and deeply-felt creation of an uncanny atmosphere, while Taymor makes an exotic foray into the formidable resources of the digital era's special effects to achieve the play's magic and enhance the strangeness of her Hawaii locations. With these plays film makers engage with the two strands of cinema that have co-existed from its earliest days: fantasy and realism, the dual abilities to show both more than meets the eye and reproduce exactly what the visible world contains.

In the English-speaking cinema, confidence in 'straight' Shakespeare as a source for screenplays was boosted during the 1990s by the success of Kenneth Branagh's *Henry V* (1989), a grittier version of the play than Olivier's, and his *Much Ado About Nothing* (1993), a romantic comedy set in a Tuscan villa and its lush surrounding countryside. Branagh's subsequent work for the cinema has included two more Shakespearean comedies, each in their own way innovative and engaging: *Love's Labours Lost*, reimagined as a pastiche 1930s musical (2000), and *As You Like It*, set among European expatriates in nineteenth-century Japan (2006). His most remarkable Shakespeare film to date is *Hamlet* (1996), set in the late nineteenth century and shot in an 'epic' widescreen format with an international cast, using the full (First Folio plus Second Quarto) text of the play – and consequently lasting over four hours. The textual choices favour the rest of the cast rather than Branagh's own performance as the Prince, giving a more expansive sense of the story's action and its world than such trimmed versions as that of Olivier or Zeffirelli (1990). Branagh's film convincingly brings together two important dimensions of the medium: the ability to look into the actors' eyes with an intimacy unavailable in most stage productions, and a (literally) wide scope of locations, settings, and physical action.

Two other films of the 1990s – *Richard III* with Ian McKellen (1995), and Baz Luhrmann's *William Shakespeare's Romeo+Juliet* (1996) – broke from the 'period drama' mould in situating their narratives in a counterfactual 1930s Britain and a vividly conceived Latin-American 'Verona City' respectively. *Richard III*, with a largely British cast, drew on McKellen's experience of a successful National Theatre production in similar vein, while Luhrmann aimed for a 'youth' market that had developed beyond that addressed by Zeffirelli. *Romeo and Juliet*, of course, has instant 'marquee recognition' through its title and *Richard III* has the support of the protagonist's historically unmerited but fictionally appealing notoriety. *Coriolanus*, directed by and starring Ralph Fiennes (2011), lacks this kind of support, but its gritty and vivid transposition of the play to war-torn former Yugoslavia give it greater immediacy and political heft than the fantasy of a fascist regime in 1930s

Britain. It compares favourably with the ersatz fascistic glamour of Rome and its politics in Julie Taymor's striking and sensational *Titus* (1999) – but after all, *Titus Andronicus* lacks the searching analysis of personality and power of *Coriolanus*.

The history of filmed and televised Shakespeare is one of productive tensions between commercial and artistic ambitions; the struggle to connect with audiences that might not find the plays (in the current jargon) 'relatable'; and the desire to do some kind of justice to an original without being subservient to it. The terms of the last of these have always been negotiable, and divergences from its Shakespearean source are often points in a production's favour. In the romantic comedy *Shakespeare in Love* (1998) the dramatist is placed appropriately enough in a theatre world that owes as much to Hollywood as to the West End or Broadway.

Allusions to Shakespeare across the varied genres of the visual media could be pursued far beyond the scope of this essay. They turn up in situation comedies like *Moonlighting*: in a 1986 episode titled 'Atomic Shakespeare', the relationship of the principal characters was reimagined in terms of *The Taming of the Shrew* as a schoolboy is forced to stop watching his favourite show to study the play. There are such glancing quotations as the final line of *The Maltese Falcon* (1941), when Sam Spade is asked what the statuette of the falcon is made of and replies with the slightly misquoted 'the stuff dreams are made of'. And in a famous commercial for lager Yorick's skull becomes a football, during a performance of the play's graveyard scene, prompting the expected comment 'I bet he drinks Carling Black Label'. Like the cinema films, from the earliest silents to the newest to reach the screen – in 2014, *Cymbeline*, by Michael Almereyda, and in 2015, *Macbeth*, by Justin Kurzel – they testify to the persistent attraction of Shakespeare's plays on screens of different sizes. Meanwhile YouTube, with its freelance videos, parodies, and reworkings of existing material, and transmissions by streaming of performance videos, are further signs of the vitality of the plays in the expanding media; and the recent television and DVD versions of productions by the RSC, Shakespeare's Globe, and the Stratford Ontario Shakespeare Festival have taken the opportunities for recorded theatrical Shakespeare to another level.

Part Two

Further Reflections

John Ashbery, Poet

As a child I was fascinated by a forbidding-looking three-volume set of Shakespeare's works that my grandfather owned. It dated probably from about 1870 and was copiously illustrated with steel engravings that frequently tended toward the lurid, even when the subject didn't. Of course I couldn't make much of the texts at such a young age, but I had Lamb's *Tales from Shakespeare* which helped. I used to go back and forth between them and the play in question, checking them against each other. I remember particularly digging into them at the age of eight (this would have been in 1935), and 'motoring' with my parents in to the nearby city of Rochester to see the Max Reinhardt film of *A Midsummer Night's Dream*, which featured such Hollywood staples as James Cagney, Dick Powell, Joe E. Brown and Olivia de Havilland in her film debut. Mickey Rooney played Puck, or rather he played Mickey Rooney playing Puck.

A mixed bag obviously, but the Mendelssohn music and dazzling cinematography overcame any objections I might have raised at that age. I hadn't thought of *Tales from Shakespeare* until a couple of months ago when I happened to write a poem with that title. That's how writing comes about for me.

Tales from Shakespeare

John Ashbery

It seemed like a huge part of our lives
revolved around the woodpile, all buzz
and splatter one minute, low wigwams the next.

He made a horse, like what was on the farm
at which end of the store they let
the young men practice. (The others dress funny.)
Kids used to hang around, queering the pitch for

the vanilla tower

following its pipsqueak editor out
into the brilliant day, of casings, undeliverable, unprogrammed
appliance scepters, more. High bleachers shut off
a section of downtown. It's a part of France,

but I don't drink at these fountains.

His sister writes back and
thick as the dust on these reports (that's
my definition anyway, all enthusiastic,

or do we have to be
or does it matter?):
Welcome to the family tree.

I am sick and tired. Startling hog
ends up in a commercial
out of the bathroom window. Thanks for the soda, Pop,
and digital power. Been wondering what it was
(and not do it on someone's time).

It was time for the rectory bells, balls, whatever.
It seemed like it to me, too. The reply
to her demandingness.

Somebody sends you a bill.
At first you want to laugh. Who said
that everything was going to be a thrill?
Just leave it. The little puffin on the green-
house steps turned around,
annoyed with everything.

OK, let's cope.

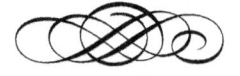

Shaul Bassi, Ca' Foscari University of Venice

On 29 March 1516 the senate of the Republic of Venice decreed that the Jews had to be confined in the former public copper foundry (il Geto), securing their economic services but keeping them safely marginalized in the city. Eighty years later the quarter was known as the Ghetto, and its cosmopolitan community had turned into a Jewish cultural hub. Nobody in that square could suspect that in a far-away city up north, a play was being staged where a fictional member of their congregation was being exhibited as a paragon of cruelty, a moneylender who could loan a thousand times more than the three ducats allowed to the real Jews of Venice.

When, in the mid-nineteenth century, the American consul W. D. Howells visited the dilapidated Ghetto, he saw the Jews (who had been emancipated by Napoleon in 1797) as ordinary citizens: 'Shylock is dead. If he lived, Antonio would hardly spit upon his gorgeous pantaloons or his Parisian coat ... he would far rather call out to him, "Ciò Shylock! Bon dì! Go piaser vederla" ["Good Morning, Shylock, nice to see you"]'. By 1938 these words would acquire an ominously different ring: 'Shylock is dead'. The Fascists' racial laws excluded all Jewish citizens from public life and paved the way for their deportation in 1943–4. Two hundred and forty-six people were deported to the death camp at Auschwitz, and only eight returned.

It is against this troubled historical background that we have decided to bring a production of *The Merchant of Venice* to the Ghetto for the first time ever, 500 years after the establishing of the Jewish quarter. This collaborative effort is not a philological or archaeological gesture; Shakespeare only portrays distant echoes of Venetian Jews, if any. Nor is it a homecoming: the fictional Shylock has in fact obscured extraordinary intellectuals such as Leon Modena or Sara Copio Sullam, who lived and died in the Ghetto. More crucially, he has played a role in the history of anti-semitism, while also opening a gateway to tolerance. Our artistic endeavour, undertaken in conversation with the local

Jewish community, does not aim at a politically correct, sanitized version of the play, but rather at an act of creative collision, one that addresses the ambivalence of the play and the place, along with their complex legacies. Today the Ghetto is a religious centre, a site of memory, a popular tourist destination, a meeting point. It is a place of questioning where we can hear Shylock's words in our ears: 'I am not bound to please thee with my answers'. (www.veniceghetto500.org)

Simon Russell Beale, Actor

I have been told that my first exposure to Shakespeare was a visit to an open-air production of *A Midsummer Night's Dream* in London. I am sure the show was delightful, but I have not the slightest recollection of it. This blank space in my mind may well be the result of my having no clearly formulated expectations of a Shakespeare play, exciting though our family outing, like many similar adventures, undoubtedly was. Mine is essentially a musical family and not a literary one; it was hoped that I would follow in my father's footsteps in becoming, at eight years old, one of those strange, semi-professional creatures – a cathedral chorister. Perhaps that is why I do have a clear memory of seeing *Don Giovanni* with my first piano teacher, which was at around the same time as I saw my first Shakespeare. Maybe I felt that I had to take an opera more seriously than a play, and listening to music was, by its nature, harder than listening to words. The truth is that I found a whole evening of Mozart both stimulating and foreign – hallucinogenic, even.

Shakespeare crept up on me unawares. Early on, I associated him with the extra-curricular, with fun, while music, which stills plays a fundamentally important part in my life, was more about a serious pressure to perform. In other words, I was introduced to Shakespeare as I think every child should be – as the result of great, relaxed teaching, and with the support of generous, open-minded and enthusiastic parents.

My first clear memory of Shakespeare was of my headmaster asking me to read aloud in class a passage from *Julius Caesar*. This was followed (or was it around the same time?) by my appearance as Hippolyta in my first school play, for which my grandmother made me a costume in ivory and gold, and which I thought was the quintessence of glamour. By then I had become seriously interested in Shakespeare's writing and in the associated thrill of acting. In retrospect it seems only natural that, immediately when I arrived at my senior school, I would seek out any chance to perform in plays – any play, but principally Shakespeare. Largely because it was thought I could sing the Willow Song, I was cast as Desdemona (with the result that I spent hours in the school library poring over photographs of Laurence Olivier and Maggie Smith in their legendary production for the National Theatre), and this was followed by King Lear when I was seventeen.

I had no idea then where all this would lead, but here I am now, thirty years into my acting career, having played King Lear as an adult, an experience of such profound significance that I would find it hard to write coherently about. For all this, I have to thank my inspired teachers, my wonderful parents and, of course, the man himself, Shakespeare, who resolutely refuses to shake off his status as the greatest playwright who ever lived.

Sally Beamish, Composer

I have always wanted to write for dance, and *The Tempest* (commissioned by the Birmingham Royal Ballet for 2016) provided a strong, visual starting-point. There are the images of the sea and the island which together carry a sound of magic. Then there's the sense of our not being sure what's real and what isn't. This led me into a mysterious, creative, and ambiguous sound world. Shakespeare puts this mystery in front of his audience, and we are not sure where he is leading us.

I draw inspiration for my music from the natural world, and from natural sounds. *The Tempest* is full of these kinds of sounds, as well as several actual songs. It is a strange and wonderful experience presenting Shakespeare without words. The voices are silent, and the bodies must express what's there. I've been working with David Bintley's vision and structure for the ballet, which has sent me back to the play and directly to Shakespeare's words.

Once you remove the singer from the songs, the composer is left with patterns and rhythms. But these are so distinctive that you can tell which song it is, even though it is now wordless. I remember setting 'Full fathom five' when I was seven or eight years old. I don't know how I found it, but it certainly appealed to me, perhaps because of the bells, which make it a little like the well-known nursery rhyme, 'Ding, dong bell'. There is something child-like about the songs that Ariel sings. We sang another setting of 'Full fathom five' at school that has also stayed with me. Years later I wrote a piece called 'Ariel' for solo viola (my own instrument) which seems to suit the character because of the graceful, troubled poignancy of its sound.

A few years ago I wrote a setting of Caliban's speech 'The isle is full of noises' for tenor and horn, and I found within the language an absolutely beautiful rhythm that led me to compose lots of unexpected phrases. That composition took me into a sound world that I'd never been to before, and it was ethereal, magical, and touching to find that a so-called monster expresses himself with such sensitivity. While working on the ballet, I embarked on a series of solo pieces related to *The Tempest*. The saxophone, as a hybrid instrument, seemed to represent Caliban. Richard Ingham, who commissioned this work, had sent me Douglas Dunn's poem 'An Address to Adolphe Sax in Heaven', but, knowing that I wanted to base the piece on Caliban, I didn't look at it. When Richard received the work, he said he admired the way I'd used the poem. It turns out that, in the second verse, Dunn compares the saxophone to Caliban. Dunn and I had both arrived at the same place but independently. For the ballet, I've evoked the sound of a saxophone by combining bassoon and horn. I've used uneven bars for Caliban, my own hybrid of 7/8 and 4/5 time, which is unusual for the dancer and provides the sense of an extra foot, or even a limp.

I have chosen to portray Prospero sometimes through horns and sometimes through cellos. There is something of a fanfare-chorale about his commanding presence. He, Miranda and Ferdinand are brought together in unity by a trio of strings. The spirits are represented by woodwind instruments.

Nothing is predictable in Shakespeare. You can look at the language through any lens you like; you still won't know what is going to happen next, and it's the same with his storylines. As a composer I allow myself to be subsumed by that uncertainty and it takes me to sound worlds I would not have discovered on my own – a beautiful land. Every time I work with Shakespeare I find I put myself out of the frame, and allow him to take the lead.

David Bintley, Director, Birmingham Royal Ballet

My first memories of Shakespeare were during a family holiday with my parents when I was about seven years old. We visited Stratford-upon-Avon and, since I was an avid reader, I borrowed a book from the library to find out more. We stayed one night, and I remember being taken to see Shakespeare's monument in Holy Trinity Church. In my early teens we read some of the plays at school, taking turns to read different roles with an enthusiastic English teacher who wanted to be an actress. Much later I enjoyed going to Stratford-upon-Avon to see the shows with my friend Cormack Rigby, the influential presentation-editor for BBC Radio 3, who, in his later years, became a Roman Catholic priest.

For 2016 Birmingham Royal Ballet is producing a brand new work: *The Tempest*. The seeds for the project were sown back in 1982 during the first full-length ballet I worked on, based on Sibelius's tone poem *The Swan Tuonela*. It was a composite which had to draw on Sibelius's other works, including his incidental music for *The Tempest*. We used the overture, but most of the music is not substantial enough for dance. Later, in thinking more about the possibility of an entire ballet based on *The Tempest*, I realized that Shakespeare's text and Sibelius's music – pine forests, plains, and very cold water – do not really go together. So the project was filed away in my bottom drawer.

Over the last few years, I began to realize that I wanted to work with the composer Sally Beamish, whose music I love, and I began to think through my portmanteau of experience. For me, ballet can communicate the structure and clarity of Shakespeare's narrative and set it in a time that doesn't have to apologize for being close to Shakespeare's own (think of how prettily Verona can be depicted in ballet versions of *Romeo and Juliet*, for example). In *The Tempest* it is impossible to do justice to the points of grievance and genuine pain that Prospero describes near the beginning, so dance needs to find a different way to portray his anger and desire for revenge. But then this turns into forgiveness, and it is as if all his magic has been really about that.

As my friend the novelist David Lodge likes to remind me, many people who turn up to watch a Shakespeare play haven't seen it before. Ballet can celebrate the simplicity of good storytelling whilst at the same time putting back the complexity of Shakespeare into the movement. A great dance actor can communicate eloquently through a single look.

Michael Bogdanov, Director

Shakespeare was boring; Shakespeare was dead; Shakespeare was a necessary slog through the tangled undergrowth of caesura, etymology, Anglo-Saxon, middle-high German, grammatical obscurity in search of the Golden A-level-English Fleece. Jason had it easy. One whole term spent on one whole Hamlet soliloquy – 'How all occasions ...' – lessons courtesy of Mr. Cowton, a Pickwickian figure given to spouting chunks of Chaucer in what he authoritatively informed us was the original fourteenth-century accent (how did he know?). As far as fifteen-year-old schoolboys were concerned (intent on smuggling copies of *Health and Efficiency* into the back-row), Hamlet's problem could be solved simply by having a good ...

But then came Richard Burton. The magical, sensational seasons of 1954–6 at the Old Vic. A school trip to see the Dane, perching on the hard 1/6d benches up in the gods. A revelation. Shakespeare was alive; Shakespeare was modern; Shakespeare was real. His language rang of the street. No filtering phrases through a pound of plums, but an electrifying Welsh twang. Burton was Burton; others were characters. But he, like another young Welshman some ten years later, Anthony Hopkins, tore the language apart and stuck it back together again in a fashion that made absolute sense even to Brylcreem-quiffed fifth-form sceptics. I went back to see him again and again – Coriolanus, Othello/Iago (alternating with John Neville), Henry V – a new hero to go alongside my discovery of Sartre and Camus. Shakespeare the conservative mutated into Shakespeare the existentialist. The readiness was all.

I decided not to study English at University (Trinity College Dublin), but opted instead for French and German (thereby giving myself a banging headache with the latter), indulging in the double-think of (a) languages being more useful, and (b) I could always read up on anything I wanted to in English. I stayed in Dublin eleven drunken years in television and theatre and, except for the odd critical excursion to see some old-fashioned ham perpetrated by the Anew MacMaster company, or the blood and thunder of a visiting Donald Wolfit, Shakespeare was noticeable for his absence. I didn't come back to Shakespeare until I was thirty.

After a run of revue, ballad concerts, show-bands, musicals and 125 programmes as producer/director for RTE (Ireland's national television company), I returned to the UK determined to immerse myself in Shakespeare. And so I became the oldest Assistant Director ever at the place where I mistakenly thought they knew more about Shakespeare than anywhere else in the world – the Royal Shakespeare Company.

Forged as I was on the anvil of my Russian father's Marxism and the Labour fire of my Welsh Valleys mother, the lack of political engagement alongside the Avon dismayed me, and, with the exception of the glorious groundbreaking exuberance of Peter Brook's *A Midsummer Night's Dream*, I did not take much from assisting a galaxy of illustrious names – except the confirmation that Will's work contained a lot more 'invisible bullets' (to borrow from Stephen Greenblatt) than we were being shown. And so, after eighteen months, I left to flex my own bardic muscles. The Wars of the Roses, Cultural Materialism and abusive letters from apoplectic colonels were all in the future.

Meanwhile, eyes bright with misunderstanding, I embarked on a quest to pluck out the political, existential heart and mystery of the plays, sometimes despairing – *As You Like It, Cymbeline, Antony and Cleopatra* – sometimes exultant – *Measure for Measure, Julius Caesar, The Taming of the Shrew, Hamlet, Romeo and Juliet*, all the Henrys and the Richards – a quest that has led me down the path of some seventy productions – from Newcastle to Leicester, from The Young Vic, back to Stratford, and then world-wide. Some plays I have returned to over and over again; *The Tempest* I have directed five times. The trouble is, I never get it more than half right. The trouble is, it's never the same half. But anyway, what is 'right'? Directing is often a case not of knowing what you want but knowing what you don't want. I shall try again ...

Kenneth Branagh, Actor and Director

My faith in Shakespeare, and in the theatre, was awoken one midsummer's morning in 1978 on the hard shoulder of the M40. I was hitchhiking to Stratford-upon-Avon, my first such solo expedition, and I was nervous. I was monstrously overburdened with the camping equipment that I had purchased on tick from my mother's Littlewoods catalogue (so much so that when I tried to climb into the high lorry cab that had kindly stopped for me, I fell backwards like a stone. A piece of physical comedy I would later use for Benedick, but without the rucksack). You will understand I was uncertain in every sense of what lay in the road ahead. I was seventeen years old.

For me at that time, Stratford-upon-Avon was a wonderland. I walked around, jaw open, surreptitiously touching old buildings and trying not to look odd, visiting everything that appeared to have a connection with the town's most famous son, and yet for all my wanderings, returning time after time after time to the theatre to stare at it from every possible angle: to gape, to dream, to wonder.

In my tiny tent each evening, I would pore over the theatre programs and reflect on the wonders of the day, marking my favourites from the shows: the great Ian Charleson as Ariel, David Suchet as Grumio, Zoe Wanamaker in everything, and this very striking girl who I noted had just left RADA, and who had a tiny part in *The Taming of The Shrew*, and magnetically scored in every second she spent on stage. I still have the penciled note that says, 'Don't forget this girl', the unforgettable Juliet Stevenson.

After four days I left Stratford, but I never left Shakespeare. Rather I carried him as a guide, as a faith forever onward. Indeed a mere six years later, when the whirligig of time had spun me through drama school and out into the world as a professional actor, I had cause to remember the wonder and the wildness of that first pilgrimage; the riot of that first evening; the way that RSC company had started the *Shrew* – with a bang not a whimper – and carried it electrically through the evening; and the language which had flowed from it. Here was Shakespeare as a faith, in action: modern, violent, messy, wondrous and humane. It was an example I took to heart when it came to my first RSC audition. And indeed I tried to put my own faith in that very quality of wildness and beauty, humanity and truth. At stake was a place in the 1984 season and a chance to be in the company of the great Antony Sher and the great Roger Rees. It seemed to me that Hotspur might be the man to help me claim a place in that august company. And, yes, in my version he had a stammer. I thought of that daft-looking kid arriving in Stratford, like a bad advert for the Boy Scouts; I thought of the greatness I had witnessed on that hallowed stage, and, as I stared out into a different, but equally thrilling darkness, I did everything I could to channel Harry Percy and his emotive exasperation as he explains to his monarch the truth behind his apparent refusal to comply with his King's wishes.

Thank God the RSC said 'yes', and from that moment, Stratford, the company there, and that theatre, offered a faith in me, which has been a humbling inspiration in all the many joyous years of Shakespeare which have followed.

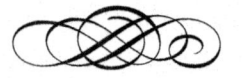

Debra Ann Byrd, Artistic Director and Actor, The Harlem Shakespeare Festival

My work with Shakespeare began in 1997 after I'd seen a troupe of black actors from the Public Theater performing his work at a special event; I was inspired to go to college. I thought the language was beautiful and intriguing. I wanted to see more. I wanted to learn how to do what I saw the actors doing: to speak the speech, and with such lovely words. I finally got my chance when I took my first Shakespeare class at Marymount Manhattan College.

Shakespeare has come to mean a lot to me. I have built my life and career around performing Shakespeare, and around providing opportunities for others to perform and study his works as well. In 2013 I founded the Harlem Shakespeare Festival, a small professional theatre festival, across Harlem, spanning late summer through to early spring. The festival brings Shakespeare scripts alive featuring three to five Shakespeare and modern plays, master-classes, panel discussions, workshops, international symposia, artist talk-backs, 'Shakespeare4Kids', 'Shakespeare in Music', 'Shakespeare on Film' and 'Shakespeare in the Open Air'.

Shakespeare is the source of my every inspiration. The excellence of Shakespeare's texts and plays inspires me to aim for excellence as well. I create wonderful theatre because I produce wonderful works by Shakespeare with a Harlem touch. I am inspired to create theatre for women – women, and especially classically-trained actors of colour. I aim for understanding and unity in the arts. I am an Artist Activist and Shakespeare is my medium.

John Caird, Director

I first got to know Shakespeare through my mother's passionate attachment to the works. She was christened Viola Mary because *Twelfth Night* was her mother's favourite play (though my mother hated the name, thinking it rather arty, and was called Mollie all her life).

As a child, she and my father took my siblings and me to Shakespeare productions in the gardens of Oxford colleges. We lived right in the centre of Oxford, so it was the cheapest and most efficient way of introducing us to the plays. I dare say the productions and the acting were pretty dodgy but I was enchanted by the stories.

Indeed, so much so that my little brother and I decided to read all the plays. I was fifteen and he was thirteen and with the obsessive pretension of over-educated teenagers, we decided we would get up on thirty-seven consecutive mornings at 5.00 a.m. to read through the entire canon, a play a day. We brewed an enormous pot of tea before we started act one and took a toast and marmalade break half way through each play – and five weeks and two days later, bug-eyed with fatigue, we finally made it to the end of *Pericles*.

My personal involvement with the plays actually started a few years before this. I attended Magdalen College School in Oxford, an all-boys school where there was a tradition of mounting Shakespeare plays. My first major role was playing Desdemona in *Othello* at the age of twelve. I still have the photographs. I'm wearing a very fetching gold headdress and my make-up is positively whorish.

The school also organized trips to nearby Stratford-upon-Avon, where I saw plays from the 400th centenary season onwards: David Warner's Hamlet, the John Barton and Peter Hall *Wars of the Roses*, and many others.

By the time I had left school, I had no doubt whatsoever that the theatre was where I wanted to be – and no doubt either that Shakespeare was what it was really all about. I have worked in the theatre ever since and, though my career has taken me all the way through the classical repertoire, through countless new plays and musicals and operas, I always return to the works of Shakespeare as my primary source of imaginative nourishment and inspiration. They are the hardest plays to direct, with the most complex characters, the densest and most beautiful imagistic language and the most profound philosophical meaning. They are never to be solved or even completely understood. Rather, they stand as the highest peak of dramatic and poetic achievement, works that teach us most truthfully what it means to be human or whether indeed there is any meaning in being human.

Antoni Cimolino, Artistic Director, Stratford Festival, Ontario

Shakespeare is like love: it's technically possible to live without any, but once you've experienced that rush in your heart, you can't settle for anything less.

I fell in love with Shakespeare at the age of sixteen. Some friends and I had gone to visit the Stratford Festival, where we got tickets for *Love's Labour's Lost*, a play I'd never even read before. By the end of the performance, my life had changed forever.

That play spoke to me, as no play had before. Four young men, in thrall to their hormones, make a rash vow of abstinence and then find they can't live up to it. As a Catholic teenager, I could relate to that.

The production was ravishingly beautiful, full of life, very funny and very sad. It dazzled me with its clarity and its truth. And as I sat there, I felt an extraordinary connection with everyone else in the theatre that day. Through Shakespeare, we were all being united in a shared experience – but one that affected us all in different ways. From that point on, I knew I wanted to work in the theatre.

The more time I've spent on Shakespeare's plays, the more I've realized that their greatness lies in the fact that they defy reduction. What is *Hamlet* about?

We've spent four centuries sifting through possible answers, and will continue to do so till the end of time. The greater a work of art, the harder it is to reduce it to a single idea. Shakespeare saw irreducible mysteries at the heart of experience, mysteries for which he resolutely refused to offer solutions. That's what makes his plays so true, and that's what informs my work as a director. Human beings aren't solvable equations. In real life, we can never really know what someone else is thinking or feeling. We can never really know who they are.

'Why, look you now, how unworthy a thing you make of me', says Hamlet to Guildenstern. 'You would play upon me, you would seem to know my stops, you would pluck out the heart of my mystery'. To me, that's the essence of Shakespeare's genius: his understanding that questions about the human heart have only one reliable answer, the one given in the film *Shakespeare in Love*: 'It's a mystery'. That's what makes Shakespeare our greatest playwright – and that, surely, is why we love him.

Wendy Cope, Poet

My first encounter with Shakespeare was a bit unfortunate. It involved the fairies in *A Midsummer Night's Dream*. There were altogether too many fairies in my early education at an all-girls school. Fairies and nature. Boring. Peaseblossom, Mustardseed, Cobweb and the other one. Imagine what Nigel Molesworth, immortal hero of *Down with Skool*, would have made of Peaseblossom and her (his? its?) mates. That's pretty much how I felt at the age of nine or ten.

The next encounter, when I was fourteen, was very different: a school outing to see Franco Zeffirelli's production of *Romeo and Juliet* at the Old Vic. Judi Dench as Juliet, John Stride as Romeo, Alec McCowen as Mercutio. I was bowled over. I went back in the school holidays to see it four more times. *Twelfth Night* was also in the repertoire, so I saw that several times as well.

A couple of years later, my parents decided that my friend Rosemary and I could be allowed to spend a few days in Stratford without any adults. This was exciting. My mother booked the hotel and the theatre tickets and off we went. We were very good sixteen-year-olds and only did what we were supposed to do, visiting the Shakespeare houses in the daytime and the theatre in the evenings. We saw three productions, including *As You Like It*, with Vanessa Redgrave as Rosalind.

By this time I was doing Shakespeare at school: *Macbeth* for O-level, *Hamlet* for A-level, both very well taught. I saw so many productions of *Hamlet* while I was in the sixth form that I haven't been able to face another one since.

My teenage passion for theatre-going has dwindled into reluctance to bother with booking expensive tickets and queueing for the toilets and the bar. I suppose all that Shakespeare in adolescence must have had some effect on me and I do still read a play from time to time. But where my own work is concerned, it is the *Sonnets*, rather than the plays, that have been important. I began reading the *Sonnets* when I began writing poems. I love them. Shakespeare taught me most of what I know about writing iambic pentameters and composing sonnets. Over the years I've often consulted him to find out what I could get away with. If anyone questions your handling of metre, it's really very helpful to know that you have Shakespeare on your side.

Gregory Doran, Artistic Director, The Royal Shakespeare Company

I missed out on Ophelia (it went to a boy in 2A) but in my third year at the Preston Catholic College, I landed Lady Anne. My Jesuit secondary school put on a Shakespeare play every year in the autumn half-term, and as an all-male establishment, the women's roles were played by the younger boys. My twin sister attended the Convent of the Holy Child Jesus, just across the street in Winckley Square, but the girls were never invited to take part.

I have a vivid memory of rehearsing the wooing scene between Lady Anne and Richard, Duke of Gloucester, on the stage in the school hall after classes, the din of a football game rising from the dark wet schoolyard below. Richard was played by a tall and strikingly handsome young man called Rory Edwards, in the second-year sixth. As this was the early seventies, most of us had haircuts like the Osmonds, but Rory had a dark glitter about him, a dash of Marc Bolan and T. Rex. I thought he was incredible; he was a sprinter, and the high-jump champion, and I was nervous at the thought of acting opposite him.

We were rattling through the keen encounter of wits, the breathless rally of praise and insult, backwards and forwards, as Richard extols Anne's beauty, attempting to excuse himself for killing both her husband and her father-in-law, and she vents her anger in a torrent of rebuke:

RICHARD
Fairer than tongue can name thee, let me have
Some patient leisure to excuse myself.

ANNE
Fouler than heart can think thee, thou canst make
No excuse current but to hang thyself.

(1.2.81–4)

They match each other phrase for phrase:

ANNE
He is in Heaven, where thou shalt never come.

RICHARD
Let him thank me that holp to send him thither,
For he was fitter for that place than earth.

ANNE
And thou unfit for any place but hell.

RICHARD
Yes, one place else, if you will hear me name it.

ANNE
Some dungeon?

RICHARD
Your bed-chamber.

(1.2.108–14)

Now Richard pulls the carpet from underneath Anne's feet by the outrageous suggestion that, having killed her husband, he now deserves a place in her bed.

As we rehearsed the scene, the fourteen-year-old boy I was began to feel light-headed. The rapid stychomythia meant that both of us were breathing fast, and getting faster, leading to the provocation which prompts Anne to spit at the hunchback murderer before her.

Chest heaving, brain swimming, I threw my head back and lobbed a gob of spittle at my poor fellow actor, who reeled back in shock, and for a moment I thought he was going to clobber me. This seemed to break all the rules. Standing there in my school blazer, and polished lace-ups, I was channelling, and at the same time suppressing, all the complicated emotions I felt.

Richard takes Lady Anne's hand, and places his ring on her finger:

Look, how my ring encompasseth thy finger:
Even so thy breast encloseth my poor heart

(1.2.207–8)

As Edwards reached for my hand, I could hardly breathe. Beyond jostling in the playground or on the pitch, touch was a rare occurrence between Catholic College boys in the early seventies. I felt faint.

'Doran', came a shout from the back of the hall, 'don't roll your eyes'. Mr Malone, the English Master, and 'producer' of the annual play, was having none of this simpering display, and the rehearsal came to an abrupt halt.

The play went ahead for its three performances, and the Lancashire Evening Post reported that despite what seemed 'an out-of-date tradition' of having the boys play the girls, 'Lady Anne was fetchingly played by G. Doran'.

So whenever the subject comes up of what it must have been like in Shakespeare's company when the boys played the girls, I have a particular insight. If no 'divine perfection of a woman', I probably looked quite convincing in my widow's weeds. I may have been 'fetching', I may not have been any good, but for me at any rate the scene was deeply charged, and just by speaking it out loud, together, it produced a crackle that, if not erotic, was certainly electric.

As a quietly spoken, polite, sports-averse teenager, I had been bullied in the dark playground of the 900-strong Lancashire school, but after *Richard III*, instead of getting worse, the bullying suddenly stopped, as if the mere fact of standing up in front of an audience and remembering the lines of Shakespeare commanded respect among my peers. And whatever else I have to thank Shakespeare for in my life, I will always be grateful to him for that.

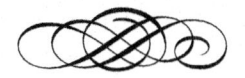

Margaret Drabble, Novelist

I discovered Shakespeare at school. The first play I remember reading in class was *The Merchant of Venice*, which I didn't (and don't) much care for, but when we moved on, to *Richard II*, *Coriolanus* and *Antony and Cleopatra*, I was enraptured, and started to read the plays by myself, for pleasure, and to learn whole scenes by heart. I also had the joy of watching Judi Dench play Ariel in the school production of *The Tempest*, and can hear her distinctive voice in that role now. Through Cambridge, where I was reading English, I remained devoted to Shakespeare, both on the page and on the stage.

At that period I longed to be an actress myself, partly because of the spell of the blank verse, and played, with varying degrees of success, Titania, Imogen and Viola. I was surrounded by undergraduates who were on their way to becoming the great classical actors of our age – Ian McKellen, Derek Jacobi, Corin Redgrave and many others whose performances remain memorable to me to this day. Clive Swift's Falstaff, directed by John Barton, with McKellen as Shallow and Jacobi as Hal, was a tour de force. It was a golden period of drama, producing performers and directors who became an important part of our theatrical heritage.

When I left Cambridge, my midsummer night's dream of becoming an actress survived a couple of seasons playing fairies and wenches at the RSC, but my career as a writer was easier to sustain, so Shakespeare came to occupy a different role in my life. He has been a continuing source of inspiration. Lines from Shakespeare run through my head every day, so it is not surprising that many of them have embedded themselves, sometimes directly, sometimes as echoes, in my fiction. His themes have haunted and perturbed and delighted me, and the texture of his language has enriched me. Although he is arguably the greatest writer in English that has ever lived, there is nothing forbidding about his genius. He does not shut us out: he welcomes us in. We thrive in his company. He is inexhaustible. It's impossible to imagine what we would have been without him, so deeply is he interwoven in the fabric of our imaginations.

Harold Bloom credited him with the invention of the human. And, in an important sense, he was right.

Dominic Dromgoole, Artistic Director, Shakespeare's Globe

Shakespeare began for me in the cot with my father steadily intoning on an iambic rhythm as he put my brother, my sister and me to sleep with favoured chunks of verse. He had for a while read Racine to us, in French Alexandrines, but the preciousness of that struck even him as excessive, so he settled into his best-loved poet. Something about the language, and the footfall, and the incoming tide of sleep impressed itself firmly on even a brain that could not understand a jot. The gentle warmth of that recital, not boomed and declaimed, not whispered and broken, but steady, and with the kind strength a parent owes a child, still feels to me as the best way to say it.

Throughout life, Shakespeare works as an emotional gymnasium, a place where we can rehearse feelings in the safe imagination of our reading or a theatre, before we encounter them in the rude actuality of life. We know about the endless wanting of love from Romeo and Juliet before we feel its frightening potential for real; we discover the identity-challenging terrors of jealousy in Othello before we suffer such pangs in the world; and we are prepared for the horrible ingratitude of society by Lear before we witness the world's inevitable turn of its back toward us. Rehearsing these feelings through Shakespeare's plays doesn't lessen the richness of the real feelings, but being prepared for our heart's capacity to hijack us does no harm.

As an artist, it is Shakespeare's restless and reckless courage that most impresses. Any artist who can come up with the caustic and acidic satire of Timon of Athens, the sheer delighted enchantment of *A Midsummer Night's Dream*, the enclosed bourgeois sitcom of *The Merry Wives of Windsor*, and the desolating, bleak sorrows of Lear, was clearly something of a shape-shifter. But it seems with Shakespeare that, every time he sat down to write, he wrote himself anew, and went on an adventure, driven by instinct and a passion for wit and truth and life, whose destination he did not really know until he put down his pen. That courage in not repeating, and in going into every situation charged with all his own knowledge and experience, but essentially naked and open, is a challenge for all of us to be as brave and as free.

People sometimes say there is too much Shakespeare. You might just as well say there is too much air.

Ellen Geer, Artistic Director of The Will Geer Theatricum Botanicum

As a child, I watched my parents perform in Shakespeare plays. I attained my Actors' Equity Union card as the First Fairy in *A Midsummer Night's Dream* aged fifteen. I learned all the young ladies of Shakespeare so I could go with my father, Will Geer, and help demonstrate when he taught.

While experiencing the blues of being a teenager with crushes, he handed me a Shakespeare book and said, 'read what he writes of love, and you'll never need a psychiatrist'. I now refer to Shakespeare's humanitarian view of the human condition on most things in life, as his words are a natural therapy.

Many people and nations use the Bible for a life resource and for examples of how to live. I use Shakespeare.

Elevated language demands elevated thoughts and movement, and thinking. In this era, it is interesting to note (as our verbal expression dwindles down with the digital world of tweets and short-cuts that exclude the eye-to-eye contact that taps the heart-to-heart communication) Shakespeare has become extremely popular.

At Theatricum Botanicum, we seek to pass on the classical stories and language of Shakespeare. Our work with the next generation is as important to us as the performances for audiences. Shakespeare is music for the soul.

Michael Holroyd, Biographer

I first read Shakespeare at school: *Julius Caesar* it was. I was greatly impressed by Antony's speech in the Forum and later tried to use his technique when chairing committees. But I was irritated by Brutus's self-conceit, especially when he was in the wrong, and I found myself using his words when losing arguments: 'Good reasons must of force give place to better'. I knew how maddening this could be.

I have encountered many Shakespeares in my biographical career, beginning with Hugh Kingsmill's subtle and imaginative playwright in his novella *The Return of William Shakespeare*. Resuscitated for six weeks in 1943, Shakespeare reads what the critics have written about him – and retaliates. Hesketh Pearson's *Life of Shakespeare* was dedicated to Kingsmill and has a charm and boldness that, Anthony Burgess wrote, were qualities 'professorial biographers are not encouraged to profess'. But Pearson (who left his copyrights to me) had the advantage of being an actor and learning much of Shakespeare by heart. This, he believed, saved his life in the First World War. Given little time to live by the doctors, he began speaking the comedies aloud in his hospital bed – and miraculously recovered. 'You have him by heart', wrote Bernard Shaw.

Shaw himself claimed to be a taller man than 'the poor foolish old Swan' whom he pretended to despise. His concealed admiration became clear to me when I wrote Shaw's biography. 'Shakespeare is a far taller man than I am', he had written, 'but I stand on his shoulders'. What he hated were the sentimental and melodramatic productions of Shakespeare by Victorian actor-managers. When I came to write a group biography of Henry Irving, Ellen Terry and their families I found myself giving the book a Shakespearean title (*A Strange Eventful History*) from Jacques's speech 'All the world's a stage' in *As You Like It*.

My biography of Lytton Strachey led to my name appearing twice in S. Schoenbaum's celebrated multiple biography *Shakespeare's Lives*. One was congratulatory when I showed Strachey looking in a mirror and seeing Shakespeare; the other was critical showing me confusing Strachey's beliefs with Shakespeare's. But my many Shakespeares have been gathered from biographical subjects, their thoughts and feelings. I see myself as a professional amateur who has found validity among scholars, actors and the general reader.

Gordon Kerry, Composer

You can hear that it's early morning in the high, spacious counterpoint of violins and violas and the distant sound of hunting horns. The four lovers awaken, one by one, each dreamily singing the name of his or her beloved. The horns get closer, the music swells; 'we are awake', they sing. Helena's 'and I have found Demetrius like a jewel', sung to a simple rising scale, is echoed by the others, and each 'jewel' is sounded on a different one of the twelve possible major triads, shimmering in the sound of harp and strings. This is music of profound transformation: after their 'mad pageant' in the wood, the lovers, temporarily enlightened, return to the real world of the Athenian court. As a young teenager, hearing, by chance, that short quartet from Act 3 of Britten's operatic version of *A Midsummer Night's Dream* on the radio one afternoon, I was transported. I realized for the first time just how magically music can interpret word and action. And it was one lesson in what a limitless source of inspiration Shakespeare has been for composers of masque, opera, incidental music or tone-poem.

The plays, of course, are full of music: the verse itself, the songs and sennets, the use of musical imagery to denote order as, in the *Dream*, when Hippolyta describes the sound of hunting hounds as 'So musical a discord, such sweet thunder'. *Such sweet thunder* was, thus, an irresistible title for the first of my three 'Shakespearean' tone-poems for orchestra. Rather than evoking any specific moment or character, it reflects some aspects of the play's atmosphere, with mysterious string textures, disembodied motives for solo instruments, glittering percussion and distant trumpet fanfares, and Mendelssohnian scurryings in and out of focus.

By comparison, *This insubstantial pageant* is series of sketches of characters and events in *The Tempest*. Given the artificial nature of the storm, I began with a short quotation from Vivaldi's *La tempesta di mare* concerto, before piling on the *Sturm und Drang* (much Neapolitan harmony!). Ferdinand mourns to a cor anglais melody. Miranda is represented by woodwinds in simple modal harmony; seeing her, Ferdinand's cor anglais finds voice again. Ariel's music is elaborated to represent the masque of Ceres, but it dissolves, violently, when Prospero remembers that Caliban is plotting against him. Caliban is 'sung' by the contrabassoon, but accompanied by (some of) his 'thousand twangling instruments'. Muted trumpets, growing softer and softer, represent Prospero's farewell.

In restless ecstasy is a fantasia on Shakespeare's noisiest play. *Macbeth* is full of thunder and lightning; ravens, 'magot-pies' and owls croak ill omens; 'drums and colours', hautboys (oboes) and trumpets are called for in the stage directions. Lady Macbeth summons her husband to murder Duncan by ringing a bell; the discovery of the murder is preceded by Macduff's knocking at the castle gate. When Macbeth's tyranny is at its height the air of Scotland is rent by shrieks, and when the invading army reveals itself before Macbeth's castle, it does so with a din of trumpets. Who could resist the sound and fury?

I evoke the witches with instruments in groups of three, often producing sounds against the use of nature. There is martial music, and a turbulent section reflecting Macbeth's battle with his conscience that is interrupted by the bell, the knocking at the gate, and the violent murder. The melody of a *trouvère* love song, *E dame jolie*, sets the scene for the banquet and appearance of Banquo's ghost. The music grows ever more frenetic before a blast of trumpets and the appearance of Macduff, represented by the hymn *Beata viscera*.

Received wisdom has it that one should not set Great Poetry to music, and it is certainly true that the long pentameter line can be a challenge. (Meredith Oakes's libretto for Thomas Adès's opera *The Tempest*, for instance, is largely in rhyming tetrameter, like many songs in the plays.) Nevertheless, I have set 'Full fathom five' for children's voices and, for the Sydney Gay and Lesbian Choir, an a cappella version of Sonnet 29. The Shakespeare setting closest to my heart, though, comes in a song cycle called *Breathtaking*, composed for soprano, four wind instruments and piano. Inevitably I was drawn to texts that celebrate breath as life, ranging from Ezekiel through various Hindu and Homeric texts. My ulterior motive was that one of my sisters had been gravely ill, and this might be a kind of sympathetic magic to keep her with us. The cycle, thus, concludes with a restrained setting of Paulina's speech from that climactic moment in *The Winter's Tale*: 'Music, awake her; strike!', with wind arabesques at the words 'Dear life'.

The magic failed; my sister died. Nevertheless it gave us great comfort when I read that speech at her funeral. Just Shakespeare's words. No music.

Graphology 4274: a *true* dream recounted

John Kinsella

I dreamt a travel agent
tried to convince me to fly
again: the lure or allure
was an airline specialising
in Transatlantic silence:

flights designed for readers
of Shakespeare quartos,
or, at a stretch, folios:
delectable silence at altitude,
with the ocean and attendant
tempests far below: floating
above the viscera of drama,
the earthiness plights plots
and language are filched from.
Come fly, fly with us:
dreamliners, prompters
of eternal tomorrows.

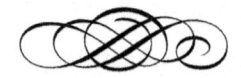

Juan Carlos Liberti (1930–2014), Painter

From the outset of my career, I chose Surrealism as my mode of expression. A world of freedom that always allowed me to develop a high degree of fantasy and creativity. Paul Klee used to say that 'Art is not about reproducing the visible, it is about making visible.' Van Gogh also revealed a similar conception when he affirmed: 'I want my paintings to be inaccurate and anomalous in such a way that they become lies, if you like, but lies that are more truthful than the literal truth.' These two concepts, reinforced by my friendship with Roberto Aizenberg and Juan Batlle Planas and my admiration for their works, became definitively incorporated in my artistic creation. Besides, I was always fascinated by the works of René Magritte, Salvador Dalí and Paul Delvaux, with whom I spent a whole afternoon in his home-studio in Brussels in 1971, viewing his magnificent works and listening to his philosophy of art.[1]

---

[1] From *Liberti: 40 Years of Surrealism* (Buenos Aires, 2006), 37.

Rafael Squirru's Shakespeare translations made me feel the rigour of Shakespeare's writing and certain surrealistic traits. I have made drawings based on *The Tempest* and *Romeo and Juliet*, as well as oil paintings and drawings based on *Hamlet*. All my painting is imaginative and the works of Shakespeare incredibly so; I always feel great inspiration when reading his works. As a painter, I mainly hope to achieve the satisfaction of seeing an image of mine well-drawn, or painted rigorously, and then wait to hear the comments of the experts.

Thank you to Carlos Drocchi and Mercedes de la Torre of the Fundación Shakespeare Argentina for supplying this contribution, which is based on a rare interview from 2011 and a quotation from a little-known publication.

'Ni un chiste ahora' (Not a joke now) by Juan Carlos Liberti. Hamlet contemplates Yorick's skull. Oil, 27.5 x 19.7 inches.

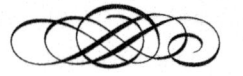

Lachlan Mackinnon, Poet

When I was fourteen we read *Macbeth* for O-Level. The dagger speech astonished me. I went around repeating it. That a hallucination could be so real not only to Macbeth but to me. To us. The words stood for something doubly imaginary. The chewy music of 'the multitudinous seas incarnadine' thrilled me. 'Multitudinous' contained crowds and crowded the line. And how unanswerable and definitive it would be to 'incarnadine'. 'Making the green one red'. I rejected the footnote's misgiving about whether 'green one' or 'one red' was meant. 'Green one' was a perfect kenning for the sea though I didn't yet have the term kenning. I am similarly sure that in *Hamlet* the flesh is 'solid' not 'sullied' because only something solid can sensibly or tangibly 'melt, / Thaw and resolve itself into a dew'. How 'resolve' suggests 'dissolve'. But we are free to choose. Perhaps we should hear both.

Since then I have studied Shakespeare, taught him and published on him. The Shakespeare I read now is not the one I first met. Neither I hope is it the last. He grows always just ahead of us. I still find that exhilarating tingle but in new places. It haunts me. In him it seems effortless.

Schiller tells us that naïve poetry is primary. Like Homer it has no ancestry. Sentimental poetry is aware of what has gone before. Part of Shakespeare's genius is to be in Schiller's sense the most intelligently sentimental of writers while at times appearing to be our greatest naïf. 'Never, never, never, never, never' uses simple repetition to name as though for the first time an absolute abandonment. Yet it called for the highest artistic cunning. That accomplishment is to envy.

Shakespeare's ethical lesson is that almost all questions have two sides. Usually though the lyric must take some sort of stand. Wanting the freedom Shakespeare grants us makes me hope my poems have room to breathe. This is a livening creative tension. And he shows how all words are equal. There is no poetic diction. There are only words which may become poetic when found right neighbours. I learn more from his plays than from his poems because of their greater linguistic range and the increasing freedom of his verse-line as he develops. And above all I am wary of imitating him. He leaves us free. He challenges us to be multitudinous.

David Malouf, Novelist

If Man is the measure of all things, then this man's mind and imagination is surely the sum of what we think of as Man.

To enter any of the plays – *A Midsummer Night's Dream*, *Romeo and Juliet*, *The Tempest* – is to breathe the air of another world, as complex and untidy, as contradictory and cruel as our own, but of another order of reality. To take in the scope of the plays, and the many worlds they open to us, is to have our consciousness extended in a new order of experience.

Shakespeare offers us the capacity, because it is already his, to enter any number of minds – a Macbeth, a Falstaff, a Rosalind, a Shylock, a Hotspur, a Caliban, a Cleopatra – and experience not only the way it works, and the peculiar language in which it expresses itself, but how, from there, the world might look; then, in a breath, to slip out of it into another.

Where does such agility of mind, and flexibility of sensory being, come from? What sort of eye does it take, what sort of ear, to render so completely all the minutiae of behaviour, and varieties of language, not only of a Hamlet, or a Beatrice or Pistol, but of a whole crowd of supernumerary ostlers, tapsters, constables, country bumpkins, household servants and highly individual but anonymous 'Boys', each one of whom insists on breaking in and being heard, and whose voices, and the shop-talk that is the daily business of their lives, still colour the language we speak and shadow the way we think and shape our feelings in it?

If you are a writer he is a wonderfully liberating influence.

He worked at a craft, a raw commercial one, and left art to find its own definition. He took the genres and the language he had inherited and remade them to accommodate what he had seen and needed to say, and over something like twenty years created an audience refined enough to appreciate and rejoice in them. He works by touch, a very Anglo-Saxon peculiarity (the French, from Voltaire to André Gide, continue to chew on their incomprehension) – allowing a place in each work for whatever energy and interest seize on and can contain; which is pretty well anything. And because he does this so completely, because his art and scope, while being inspiring and invigorating, so clearly exceed our own, he grants us permission; allows us not to be intimidated and silenced, as we might so easily be, by our limits.

Javier Marías, Novelist

After a more or less obligatory first reading of the great masters of the past, usually in our youth, many of us writers feel somewhat uneasy about revisiting them. It tends to be a rather discouraging, not to say frustrating, experience. The novelist or poet picks up a copy of Shakespeare or Cervantes, Montaigne or Hölderlin, Keats or Conrad or Proust, and after re-reading a few pages, thinks: 'What on earth am I doing here at my typewriter or computer? What is the point of me adding a single line to what they have already said?' Re-reading the classics can be an invitation to silence.

I experience this feeling myself with quite a few writers, although not with Shakespeare, who should perhaps be the one author guaranteed to have the most depressing, paralysing effect. Instead, I always find revisiting his work stimulating and enriching. It doesn't invite me to silence at all, but urges me on to write 'a little more'. How can that be? It would be absurd for anyone to compare himself with Shakespeare, to compete with or even slavishly imitate him. One takes his undoubted superiority for granted. Yet far from discouraging me, his work encourages and fills me with a desire to write, and the reason for this is that his texts are so mysterious, even when they appear not to be, and seem easy to understand – at least initially. There are so many ideas that he merely noted in passing, but left unexplored; as you travel through his plays, you notice so many sidestreets going off to left and right that you feel tempted to go down them, to venture off along paths he merely signalled, but did not take, those, so to speak, that he rejected or abandoned.

Seven of my books have titles that quote from or paraphrase Shakespeare: the novels *A Heart So White*, *Tomorrow in the Battle Think on Me*, *Dark Back of Time*, *Your Face Tomorrow* and *Thus Bad Begins*, the volume of stories *When I was Mortal* and the collection of essays *Seré amado cuando falte* (*I Shall be Lov'd When I am Lack'd*). If we look at the lines from *Macbeth* from which the first title comes: 'My hands are of your colour; but I shame / To wear a heart so white', the meaning of the word 'white' is by no means unambiguous. Does it mean 'pale' or 'cowardly' or 'innocent' or 'without stain'? If we look at the line from *Hamlet* that I've used as the title for my most recent novel: 'Thus bad begins, and worse remains behind', the Spanish characters who quote these words take them to mean 'and worse is left behind', and yet many Shakespearian exegetes and translators interpret it as meaning 'and worse lurks or waits behind' or 'worse is yet to come'. Shakespeare's ambiguity is there even in some of his most famous and often-repeated lines. We are all familiar with Othello's soliloquy spoken just before he kills Desdemona, which begins thus: 'It is the cause, it is the cause, my soul!' Almost no one bats an eyelid or pauses when they read or hear this and what follows, and yet it isn't at all clear what Othello is referring to, because he doesn't say 'This is the cause' nor, of course, 'She is the cause'. And what exactly does 'In the dark backward and abysm of time' mean, when the word 'backward' doesn't even appear to be a noun strictly speaking? And are Prince Hal's words to his pal Poins any clearer: 'What a disgrace is it to me to remember thy name! or to know thy face tomorrow!' (I, of course, gave this a contradictory twist in my novel *Your Face Tomorrow*.)

The extraordinary thing about Shakespeare is that we don't even notice the often-enigmatic nature of his words, which don't get in our way when it comes to 'understanding' what we're reading. They don't slow us down, they don't appear cryptic or abstruse. We have a sense that we're capturing everything he says without any difficulty at all. And yet, if you stop and re-read, if you look closely, you often find that while you may have 'understood', you haven't entirely 'comprehended'. The energy, the rhythm, the glow of his images and metaphors, all drive us on, and create in us an illusion of intuition, revelation, or even sudden wisdom. Then, when you emerge from the wave and look back, you realize that there is still much to explore, to develop, to puzzle over and think about. What further encouragement does an author need to write a little more?

Translated from the Spanish by Margaret Jull Costa

Yukio Ninagawa, Director

I have had an almost megalomaniac desire to 'grasp' the whole world as a theatre director. What I have been interested in is not the theatre of the portion or part but that of the whole.

In 1974, I was asked to direct *Romeo and Juliet* by Tōhō, one of the biggest entertainment companies in Japan. Up until then my theatrical activities had been limited to the field of little theatres that grew up in the late sixties. Ironically enough my career as a Shakespeare director started with Franco Zeffirelli's turning down the first offer from Tōhō.

Actually, before *Romeo and Juliet* I planned to produce and direct *Hamlet* with Kenichi Hagiwara, a popular rock singer known by the nickname Shōken, in the title role. Though the project did not materialize, I remember what gave me the idea to direct the play. Probably in 1973, a Japanese translation was published of *Rabelais and His World* by Mikhail Bakhtin. When I read it, I was seized with a kind of dreadlike amazement. I was awe-struck by Bakhtin's rich and profound outlook on the world and human beings, evident in his analysis and interpretation of the stories of Gargantua and Pantagruel in the context of their historical and social background. I think the impact of the book made me turn towards Shakespeare. Bakhtin mentions Shakespeare many times. It struck me that 'Shakespeare's the thing' to embody the ideology and attitudes expressed in the book in the form of theatre.

When the reconstruction of the Shakespeare's Globe was completed in 1997, I was appointed one of the Associate Directors of the theatre. What impressed me most upon my first visit there was its structure. The moment I stepped into the auditorium, it struck me as a mirror image of the basic structure of Shakespeare's plays: there are people of the lower class – the common people – intellectuals, nobles, and the king at the top of the hierarchy. I thus re-acknowledged the fact that the whole world is contained in Shakespeare. If you take up Shakespeare, you can have the entire world.

Since the *Romeo and Juliet* of 1974, I have directed numerous plays of Shakespeare, including *NINAGAWA Macbeth*, my localized version of the Scottish tragedy set in the samurai world of Japan's Azuchi-Momoyama era. I have made eight different *Hamlet*s, two versions of *Macbeth*, and three versions of *Romeo and Juliet*. In 1998, Saitama Arts Theatre, in Yono-Honmachi in Saitama Prefecture, launched a new project called Sai-no-Kuni Shakespeare Series, with the prospect of producing the whole canon, and, as the Artistic Director of the project, and later that of the theatre itself, I have produced thirty plays, which means seven plays are left to go. The most recently presented Shakespeare under my direction was *Richard II* in April 2015. It was performed in the main house of the Saitama Arts Theatre, but not in the usual way. The auditorium was closed and the audience was led onto the stage from the back where they found the banked seating surrounding the rectangular acting area on three sides. At the beginning of the play, more than thirty old men and women, in formal Japanese kimonos and in wheelchairs, appeared from the dark upper-stage. The same number of young people, also wearing formal kimonos or tailcoats, were pushing them. It seemed as if an enormous wave was surging swiftly and silently downstage. The old actors were members of the Saitama Gold Theatre, and the young ones were from the Saitama Next Theatre. Both these companies were my brainchildren. On cue, the old ones left their wheelchairs, and the old and the young started to mingle and chatter with one another. When the tango music that had been faintly audible in the background suddenly reverberated loudly, the whole area became filled with the couples dancing together, young with old. In Act 3, Scene 2, when Richard returns from Ireland and lands on the Wales coast, I had the floor area totally covered with a vast sheet like a wave, a light silk cloth with wave-patterns of blue, black and white painted on it as commonly used in Kabuki performances. Several stagehands held the lists of the sheet and moved it slowly up and down so that it appeared to inhale and exhale the air. From a slit in the middle of the sheet Richard appeared, a very figurative way of depicting his return from the Irish expedition. In the deposition scene, I had the crown, thrown by Richard onto the floor, fly to the head of Bolingbroke using transparent fishing coil.

Thanks to Shakespeare's language, images came to my mind one after another while directing this play, making me feel free for some reason. Shakespeare always liberates me. No other playwright has ever made me feel like that. It is as if he is telling me to do anything I like.

I am glad I met Shakespeare.

Translated from the Japanese by Kazuko Matsuoka

Janet Suzman, Actor, Director and Writer

In the hot classroom of a girls' school in Johannesburg, converted into a theatre for the occasion by adding a crude platform and squeaky curtains to the one end, and opening up the folding doors at the other to admit fond and sweating parents, I tasted the dubious delights of Shylock – aged about thirteen, I think. Cotton-wool beard badly stuck on, some kind of burnous-y, itchy garment chucked over the school-tunic, and lots of wild gestures: 'An oath, an oath, I have an oath in heaven', I yelled, and then, realizing with a blinding shame (or more probably my poor parents') that I had forgotten to remove my glasses, whipped them off and hurled them in the general direction of the wings as a gesture of defiance – and, I thought, high drama. I recall a tiny whimper from that direction as they landed on some poor girl's forehead as she skulked in the dark wing. Thus did I make acquaintance with Shakespeare.

A year later I was in the hands of a superb English teacher who clearly was cut out to play a lanky Rosalind herself, and I entered the magic purlieus of the Forest of Arden. Thus that magic casement was opened enough to make a young mind enchanted. We are all indebted to our teachers, and I had great luck with mine, without whom I might not have become so magnetized by language.

Is it any wonder that I got myself into drama school when I graduated from my politically tumultuous university, happy to explore the unmatched world of rich characters that Shakespeare creates?

Little did I realize, too, that his world is a tumult of politics, and that the dangers and extremities that his people find themselves in suited my whetted imagination to a T.

I have loved Shakespeare for ever so long, and haven't tired of his mysteries yet, choosing now to write about him rather than playing him, since I have been blessed with a career that has taken in so many of his creatures. I remain intrigued by the extent to which many of his female creations show an independence of spirit quite at odds with the strictures put upon them in the reality of his own times. I am in a state of continual astonishment at the modernity of his insights. Genius of his sort is obsessively fascinating.

Viva Shakespeare!

Salley Vickers, Novelist

I have taken Shakespeare as my artistic model, if that doesn't sound too inflated. I don't mean I can match our greatest writer in talent but his habit of taking an old story, and recreating it for his own, is one that I have pressed into service. There are several things about this habit of Shakespeare's that I like. One important one is that it revitalizes an old story while preserving it in contemporary consciousness. Old stories tend to enshrine abiding truths about human existence. If they are kept alive, and made new, they act as connections with our past, linking apparently disparate historical times to the present. This in turn emphasizes the degree to which all human beings, however apparent their differences, are kin. But also, the practice removes the problem of having to be original, at least where plot is concerned. I wouldn't want to suggest that Shakespeare was lazy – his rapid output at various points in his working life gives that possibility the lie. But I suspect that, like me (and here may be the inflation), he preferred to keep his originality for other things. Not having to invent a plot removes a huge artistic burden.

In *Miss Garnet's Angel*, for example, I appropriated the ancient tale of Tobias and the Angel, first written down in the Apocryphal Book of Tobit, but almost certainly passed on orally from the time of the first Jewish holocaust in 722 BC, when the Assyrians conquered Israel, taking ten of the twelve tribes of Israel into exile. Taking my cue from Shakespeare I retell the story in a contemporary vein, with the Archangel Raphael making an angelic appearance via his pictorial representations in Venice.

In my second novel, *Instances of the Number Three*, I conscript Shakespeare more overtly, by using *Hamlet*, and especially the Ghost, as a blueprint. The ghost of a dead man is central to my story. But I reverse the tragic movement of *Hamlet*. Rather than returning from the dead to urge revenge my ghost comes back to seek forgiveness.

In two of my short stories I go further and steal two of my hero's characters: the orphaned Indian child from *A Midsummer Night's Dream* and Mamillius from *The Winter's Tale*. We don't know much for sure about Shakespeare but I have an idea that he would have found this theft amusing. Anyway, I comfort myself that this is the case.

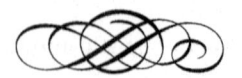

Rowan Williams, Theologian and Poet

Shakespeare is a haunted writer: the same themes run through the entire vast universe of his writings – gender confusions; lost siblings, especially twins; fathers and daughters; images or shadows and substances, especially how power is imaged and imagined. But it would be a very stupid reader or viewer who found this repetitive. What's struck me consistently since I started reading Shakespeare at school is the way in which this 'recycling' of motifs becomes a sort of philosophy in itself: human relations, human identities, human forms of speech are never exhausted in one go or indeed any number of goes. We don't come to the end of persons or their words. *King Lear* ends horribly, and Shakespeare, instead of avoiding or concealing the horror, asks what *else* might be true or possible about fathers and daughters, whether lethal miscommunication is fated to happen or if it is miraculously possible for speech to be recreated across the worst kinds of loss (Leontes and Perdita, Pericles and Marina). Royal power is sought violently and transgressively by Macbeth (or even Bolingbroke), and Shakespeare, instead of simply offering justifications for a status quo, asks what would it mean for such power to be freely abandoned; how authority, in stepping aside from its most obvious forms, renouncing independence, brings both death and unexpected life (Cymbeline; Prospero, Caliban, Ariel – Prospero, naked at his 'ending', having liberated, pleading for liberation).

I realize how much my long fascination with the question of how thinking about language itself converges with thinking about the inexhaustible elusiveness of God owes to the constant absorption of Shakespeare's imagination since my teens. Not coming to the end of things; the nakedly and uncompromisingly tragic never qualified but just *followed* by another kind of narrative; image and contrivance telling more of the truth than would-be literalism; power turned inside-out – all these things have engaged me as a theologian throughout my working life, but also, in a different mode, as a poet. St Thomas Aquinas describes contemplation as a circular motion of intellect. Shakespeare is contemplative in that sense at least, and the cause in others of contemplation, the recognition that there is always more to see and sense.

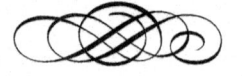

Lisa Wolpe, Director and Actor

As the Producing Artistic Director of the Los Angeles Women's Shakespeare Company for the last twenty years, I have been able to put together many world-class multicultural productions of Shakespeare in which women played all the parts, male and female. Clearly, as Gertrude and Ophelia together have 350 lines of text, and Hamlet has nearly 1,500 lines, the greatest share of glorious philosophical inquiry goes to the melancholy Prince. As an actor I've played many wonderful female characters, but my greatest triumphs have been in portraying Hamlet, Richard III, Angelo, Romeo, Iago, Shylock – all expansive, fascinating male roles; brilliant, complex characters created by the best writing in the world. Becoming each of these brilliant, princely, flawed, loving, conflicted male characters provided a cornucopia of learning opportunities. Having a role to work on worthy of an artist's full intellectual and emotional scope is the greatest gift to any actor's growth. Currently I am touring my solo show, 'Shakespeare and the Alchemy of Gender', internationally. It's a piece in which I play both male and female characters, and it is both profoundly personal and fiercely political. My intent is to build empathy and compassion by using Shakespeare to explore themes of violence and forgiveness. One walks in the shoes of the opposite gender to explore the unknown and make at least small steps toward understanding others. I have spent many years working on cross-gender Shakespeare. Globally, there is a strong resurgent interest in this ancient art form.

Gender bending is, of course, written into the Shakespeare plays, which were originally performed by all-male companies. The Alchemical goal of self-knowledge was represented as an androgynous ideal in Elizabethan theatre. And yet, at the time, women were not allowed to write for, or play on, public stages. Even in relatively recent theatrical history, when I first started working as an actress, the availability of interesting roles for women in

Shakespeare seemed to be very limited. Disempowerment on every level raises the question: 'How are you going to find your artistic and political voice?'

The many all-female productions I have helmed have offered women unique opportunities to shine. Our mission has been to bring women's voices onto the stage and into the world, and I believe that our work can now be considered a cornerstone in a worldwide trend of interest now building for gender-bent productions of Shakespeare. As a director, I have been able to open many pathways for new voices by cross-gendering and re-gendering certain characters to explore questions of gender and identity.

At one point women were not allowed to play on public stages; it was commonly believed that women did not have a soul, that their minds lacked retention. When I was young, women who were actresses could expect to be offered the archetypal roles of girlfriend, wife, whore, mother, victim – but very little else seemed to be available to a woman. People of colour generally could not hope to play more than a servant's role. Now, a simple male/female binary is no longer sufficient for an exploration of gender, nor does one base the performance of identity in today's theatre on the colour of one's skin. Many young and passionate artistic souls are willing courageously to carry Shakespeare's gorgeous words into a new era, and are holding 'the mirror up to nature' with a beautiful authenticity. We are all the richer for researching and presenting more about one another and the infinite variety of our humanity onstage, and for creating Shakespearean productions that reflect both our growing self-awareness and our global awareness of shared community and culture.

Internationally, the great Shakespearean questions – that present men and women as not being what they seem to be on stage – remain extremely relevant. Old ideas of behaviour and gender expectations are being replaced by a new performative agency quite beyond a white-male-dominated, cisgender binary. The theatre of the future is sure to continue to mine the classics whilst at the same time opening up our stages to a brave new world of practitioners, who have much to say about performing identity and gender onstage.

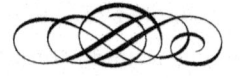

Greg Wyatt, Sculptor-in-Residence, the Cathedral Church of St John the Divine, New York City

By the time I was twelve years old, I had begun to take drawing seriously. I would draw still-life and, although I had no knowledge of anatomy, I did have a clear sense of figures in context, in architecture, and of the built environment around a subject. When I was thirteen, I travelled to Mexico with my family to some of the Mayan archaeological sites and into the rain forests of the Yucatan. We saw the great Aztec pyramids of the sun and the moon, and then travelled through the jungles to see art from earlier periods. This is how and where sculpture really started for me. Seeing the art of these different cultures changed what I wanted to draw. I became aware of three-dimensions and started to draw sculptures. My early inspiration came from the cornstalk, stelae figures, often in dance-like poses. I started to work on terracotta sculpture and, while a student of Art History at Columbia College, I also learnt about human anatomy. Especially, I became fascinated with Mayan art and its relationship between text and figures.

When I first encountered the possibilities of reading Shakespeare's poetry as a teenager, and because of our travelling in the Yucatan, there existed in my mind a very strong visual arts influence. All this has supported my own Shakespeare research drawings and *cire-perdue* ('lost wax casting') maquettes for my eventual bronze monuments presented in homage to Shakespeare in the Great Garden of New Place in Stratford-upon-Avon.

It's Shakespeare's similes, metaphors and boldness of imagery that catch my attention. My quest is to discover how poetry can be expressed through the plastic arts. When beginning work on a new Shakespeare-inspired sculpture, I take a word at a time and draw what particular words mean to me. All of my pieces begin life as a series of maquettes, which themselves come from those initial drawings. I don't set out to depict characters in individual plays, but rather to express impressions of what a Shakespeare play presents to my mind's eye, how the ideas of the play can take on physical form.

The Winter's Tale in the Great Garden, for example, takes as its inspiration the line 'be stone no more', which to me presents the whole process of making a bronze, from wax model through to its final casting. There is a correlation between the fluidity of creating a bronze and Hermione herself coming to life, being re-engaged with life, stepping out from stone and into warmth. Julio Romano, the Italian painter whom Shakespeare mentions in *The Winter's Tale*, was well known for his engravings based on oil paintings. As I imagined him taking away the paint and transposing what he saw onto a metal plate, I realized I was embarked on a similar process, but in my case I was removing the play-text and transposing its essence into bronze.

Tactility is the by-word for the sculptor. When working on *King Lear*, I gave the central figure an enlarged ear. This became the place for the Fool, whose quiet, insistent, whispering words began to influence my evocation of Lear's facial expressions.

Sculpture allows the arrested moment to compel, question, and captivate a viewer's attention. In a way, it is like a moment of performance, frozen in time, which draws us in. For me, working as a sculptor with Shakespeare means stepping inside his words, committing his lines to memory, and then acting them out – 'bodying them forth' – in sketches, clay, wax, maquettes and bronze.

'**The Winter's Tale**' *by Greg Wyatt, bronze, h. 8 ft 9 in. The Great Garden of New Place, Stratford-upon-Avon.*

'King Lear' *by Greg Wyatt, bronze, h. 7 ft 6 in. The Great Garden of New Place, Stratford-upon-Avon.*

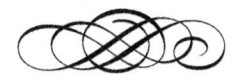

Shakespeare's Legacy of Storytelling

Indira Ghose

In a clip released by the White House on 1 April 2015, President Obama turned to the camera and drawled in faux-Southern accent, 'This is not Frank Underwood. This is Barack Obama. Frank learned it from me.' Obama was referring to the spectacularly popular Netflix series, *House of Cards*, in which Kevin Spacey, who plays the President of the United States, is fond of sharing his thoughts with the audience by means of direct camera address. The joke lies in a real president mimicking a fake president and seeming to engage with him in a tussle over who has better control of the media. There is also a sly hint that Obama is mocking the lunatic fringe of his critics who rave about his being a diabolical schemer, on a par with the fictive president in the series. As both Obama and the makers of *House of Cards* know, the idea of a Machiavellian politician drawing the audience into a cosy, complicitous relationship with him was first used to devastating effect in Shakespeare's *Richard III*. Obama is right: he didn't learn it from Underwood. He learned it from Shakespeare. The Elizabethan audience was very partial to theatrical games with illusion and reality, and relished the ironies of life imitating art. They would likely have enjoyed Obama's little quip.

Four and a half centuries later, Shakespeare still provides copy for jokes. In Shakespeare's time, the cultural resources he mined were the classics. The Humanist movement had made education, and in particular works from Classical antiquity, available to a far wider swathe of society than in the past. Grammar school students were put through a rigorous curriculum of Latin texts, culminating in Ovid and Virgil. Despite, or perhaps because of, the official view that Virgil was more valuable since he inculcated the right civic duties, Shakespeare and his peers much preferred to quarry Ovid's *Metamorphoses* for its riveting stories. Imitation was the name of the game – Ovid himself took his collection of myths from the Hellenistic poets. One lesson Shakespeare learned from Ovid was that what counted was not content but how stories were told, re-told, and adapted. Ovid was a master of self-conscious narrative, drawing attention to the very act of storytelling. Sometimes his characters tell their own stories, sometimes they relate other stories. Sometimes stories nestle within stories: in Book 10 Orpheus tells a series of tales, including that of Venus and Adonis, in which Venus herself recounts another story. His tales of gods and heroes circulated round the themes of desire, violence, and mutability, but his real interest lay in exploring aspects of his own art. Indeed, many of his characters are artists: Pygmalion, a sculptor, Orpheus, a singer, Arachne, a weaver. Shakespeare's contributions to cultural life are myriad, far too many to discuss within the scope of this essay. But one of the reasons for Shakespeare's enduring significance is that he helped shape the way we tell stories, partly through his irreverent use of narrative and literary sources, and partly through his pervasive use of irony.

Traces of Ovid are visible everywhere in Shakespeare's work. In the case of *Romeo and Juliet* and *A Midsummer Night's Dream* he actually used the same material twice – first as tragedy, then as farce, as Marx would observe about the way historical narratives repeat themselves. The story of star-crossed lovers, whose attempt to defy their families and fate ends tragically, provided material for both Shakespeare's tragedy set in Verona and for the hilarious 'Pyramus and Thisbe' episode in *A Midsummer Night's Dream*. He was deeply interested in playing with generic norms. When Shakespeare mines other sources for his work, he frequently deflates conventions. In *Troilus and Cressida*, for instance, the heroes of antiquity are exposed as either vain and narcissistic or sly and manipulative. Most notoriously, Shakespeare threw overboard the happy ending of *The True Chronicle of King Leir*, the anonymous play on which his tragedy is partly based, turning it into one of the bleakest testimonies of human despair. Generations of critics never forgave him.

In one of the lighter moments in Vishal Bhardwaj's *Hamlet* adaptation, *Haider* (2014), set in a 1990's Kashmir ravaged by bitter civil strife, the lead character introduces the term 'chutzpah' to his treacherous boyhood friends, Salman 1 and Salman 2, who, in a wink to Tom Stoppard's *Rosencrantz and Guildenstern Are Dead* (1966), are not the brightest of youths. Haider is explaining his strategy of sly resistance to the authorities in power in Kashmir. But the episode is also a comment on the film's audacious exploitation of the authority of Shakespeare's text. When moderns use Shakespeare for their own purposes, boldly, creatively, and sometimes defiantly, they are employing strategies they learned from Shakespeare. In James Joyce's *Ulysses* (1922) Stephan Dedalus unpacks his theory of *Hamlet*, while Joyce uses the play as a model for his character's quest for a father. W. H. Auden's long poem *The Sea and the Mirror* (1944) picks up where *The Tempest* ends, and offers the poet a framework within which to muse on art and life. Samuel Beckett attempts to outdo *King Lear* in his own post-apocalyptic play, *Endgame* (1957). In *Une Tempête* (1969), the Caribbean anti-colonialist writer Aimé Césaire turns *The Tempest* into a parable about imperialism. Stoppard takes two insignificant characters from *Hamlet* and makes them the antiheroes of his existentialist play, *Rosencrantz and Guildenstern Are Dead*. In *My Own Private Idaho* (1991), the filmmaker Gus Van Sant has set Shakespeare's second Henriad in the rent-boy scene in Portland, Oregon. Bhardwaj has used *Hamlet* to launch a devastating critique of Indian military rule and human rights violations in Kashmir, and the Netflix series *House of Cards* melds *Richard III* and *Macbeth* to create a scathing satire of Washington politics.

In T. S. Eliot's 'The Love Song of J. Alfred Prufrock' (1917) the speaker draws on *Hamlet* to point to his own mediocrity. Rather than taking centre stage in his own story, Prufrock insists that he is a character on the side-lines, like Polonius, or an Elizabethan jester:

No! I am not Prince Hamlet, nor was meant to be;
Am an attendant lord, one that will do
To swell a progress, start a scene or two,
Advise the prince; no doubt, an easy tool,
Deferential, glad to be of use,
Politic, cautious, and meticulous;

Full of high sentence, but a bit obtuse;
At times, indeed, almost ridiculous –
Almost, at times, the Fool.

In truth, Hamlet himself is insecure about his identity, and plays a series of roles – scholar, faithful son, revenger, friend, lover, madman – in search of his core self. The play does not contain a fool (except a dead one, Yorick, and the two clownish gravediggers); accordingly, the prince adopts 'an antic disposition' (1.5.180) to enable him to fire a volley of truths at his enemies. Around the same period Shakespeare developed the stage figure of the wise fool – a figure who was part fool, part philosopher, and whose main function was to hold up a mirror to the folly of others. With a mixture of nonsense and reason the wise fools destabilize the values of various characters – and include themselves in their incessant mockery of humanity.

Hamlet is often seen as the first modern literary subject, torn by doubt and intent on examining his inner self. Shakespeare's fools demonstrate traits of modernity, too. Detached from all social bonds, figures like Feste in *Twelfth Night* or the Fool in *King Lear* are distanced commentators on the action of their plays. Their favourite device is playing with words: as Feste puts it, 'A sentence is but a chev'ril glove to a good wit – how quickly the wrong side may be turned outward!' (3.1.11–13). Lear's Fool plays incessant games with the word 'nothing' to make Lear aware of the abyss yawning at his feet as a result of his rash behaviour: 'Thou hast pared thy wit o'both sides and left nothing i'the middle' (1.4.178–9). One of the ways Shakespeare is different from his fellow dramatists is that his range of humour includes the wryly sceptical worldview of the some of the greatest thinkers of his age: Erasmus and Montaigne. The irony that suffuses his work has become a hallmark of modernity.

It was Montaigne, in his essay 'On Democritus and Heraclitus', who gave a further twist to the Aristotelian dictum that what distinguished humankind from other species was our ability to laugh: 'Our specific property', he declared, 'is to be equally laughable and able to laugh'. Humankind is inherently ridiculous. The idea that the world might be a huge joke – and that the joke is on us – was one that the Romantics picked up and made their own. The

German literary critic, Friedrich Schlegel, developed the concept of cosmic irony. For the Romantics, Shakespeare was the greatest exemplar of irony. In addition to the scepticism that the fools articulate, what creates his sense of irony is his refusal to present or portray a single truth: instead, a multitude of stories throng each play. Antithetical, often incompatible, perspectives jostle with each other, undercutting any claims to represent the whole truth.

In the comedies, sub-plots peopled by low-life characters shed a mocking light on the values of the main protagonists, either by presenting radically different ways of seeing the world, or by showing them copying their betters. The way Launce (in *The Two Gentlemen of Verona*), Dromio of Syracuse (in *The Comedy of Errors*), and Touchstone (in *As You Like It*) manage their amorous affairs parodies the high-flown rhetoric of the wellborn lovers in the plays – as Touchstone bluntly puts it, he is joining 'the rest of the country copulatives' (5.4.54–5) mainly because human needs must be fulfilled. Even in *Romeo and Juliet*, which has become a monument to young love, the romantic passion of the lovers is set side by side with the coarse, earthy views of the Nurse and the cynical attitude of Mercutio. In *Two Gentlemen*, Launce's dog, who disgraces his owner with his lack of manners, actually behaves no worse than the gentlemen of the play, who betray their closest friends and threaten the women they love with rape. Launcelot Gobbo, in *The Merchant of Venice*, is (briefly) torn between loyalty to Shylock and attraction to the smart set represented by his new master, Bassanio – which is more than one can say of the callow young men of the play. They feel no compunction at breaking their vows to their newly-wedded wives, or humiliating the Jew once they have triumphed over him. In *As You Like It* the pastoral fantasies of the courtiers are set against the hard life of real shepherds that Corin describes, while Touchstone's boast of the superiority of courtly life makes it sound suspiciously similar to life in the country (3.2.52–65). It is not just the fools who send up the ideas trumpeted by the main characters. Clowns and rogues like Bottom (*A Midsummer Night's Dream*), Dogberry (*Much Ado About Nothing*), Pompey and Barnardine (*Measure for Measure*), Parolles (*All's Well That Ends Well*), Thersites (*Troilus and Cressida*), or Autolycus (*The Winter's Tale*) all offer counter-perspectives to the lofty thoughts (if not deeds) voiced by the aristocratic characters in the main plot of the plays.

Sometimes it is the sheer brilliance of Shakespeare's plotting that seems to demystify dominant worldviews. In *King Henry IV*, Part 1, the scene switches between the court and lowlife settings such as the Eastcheap tavern, which the young Prince is fond of frequenting. The shifts between the different locales suggest that both groups of characters are not very different in substance. The ambush of the pilgrims on Gad's Hill is a scaled-down version of the robbery of territory and treason in which those in power indulge. The change in perspectives is reinforced by the most subversive figure in the play: Falstaff. In a genre purporting to celebrate the glorious history of England and its charismatic rulers, the fat knight pauses before a crucial battle to reflect, 'What is honour? A word' (5.1.133–4). All the military heroics in the world would not replace a single human life. Falstaff's cynicism punctures the mystique of power that pervades the plays.

Occasionally all it takes is a single scene to sabotage the tragic heroism a play seems to endorse. In *Macbeth*, a drunken porter lurches onto the stage with a rambling monologue on impotence and other failings brought about by drink. This brief moment, shocking in its vulgarity and banality, and immediately following the bloody assassination, serves to debunk the ethos of violence and masculinity that dominates the rest of the play. As the philosopher Hegel pointed out, tragedies are always built around a collision of values – in the case of Macbeth, the values of loyalty to his king and overweening ambition – but Shakespeare goes further than most dramatists in presenting opposing standpoints. His tragedies end on a note of profound ambivalence – regret at what the critic A. C. Bradley in his book *Shakespearean Tragedy* (1904) called tragic 'waste', but also conflicting emotions about the protagonists themselves. The dispute about whether Othello, for instance, is redeemed at the end of the play and regains his noble stature, or is simply a grandstanding egoist, has been a bone of contention for at least a century. Even the comedies, conventionally expected to end on a note of joyful reconciliation, are permeated with wistfulness. Some characters explicitly refuse to join the revels – as Jacques puts it, he is 'for other than for dancing measures' (*As You Like It*, 5.4.191). Shylock is excluded from the merriment of the last act of *The Merchant of Venice*, Don John flees in *Much Ado About Nothing*, and, in *Twelfth Night*, Antonio and Malvolio are left out in the rain. That play ends with Feste singing a song about the wind and the rain, reminding the audience that mortality is only temporarily banished from the Arcadian landscapes of the comedies. If the comic endings are exuberant, it is because they invite both delight and scepticism about their self-consciously fragile happy resolutions.

How Shakespeare tells stories had a profound impact on creative practice and might constitute one of the main legacies he has left us. Never again would stories be told as if there were only one way to tell them. What is missing in his plays is moral closure: the plays resist the attempt to deliver a didactic message. Instead, they appeal to the autonomy of spectators, requiring them to draw their own conclusions. It is precisely this quality of multifacetedness that makes Shakespeare so amenable to reinterpretation – and that has allowed writers, directors, and artists to appropriate him for their own purposes, political or otherwise.

What Shakespeare has also left us is a treasure trove of unforgettable characters. He had the unique gift of entering into the minds of a vast array of different people across all ages and social ranks. In a letter to his brothers written in 1817, John Keats coined the term 'negative capability', defining it as the ability 'of being in uncertainties, mysteries, doubts, without any irritable reaching after fact and reason'. For Keats, the sensitivity of an artist to the world implied being receptive to all aspects of life. It precluded one thing: judgement. Shakespeare's burning curiosity about people enabled him to conjure up the lives of others. In contrast to the cardboard figures of medieval drama, the most memorable characters in Shakespeare are individuals. They display an entire gamut of often-contradictory elements. They include seductive villains like Iago or Richard III and magnetic and ruthless leaders – the audiences of *King Henry IV*, Parts 1 and 2, for instance, have long been divided into two camps, Prince Hal-lovers and Prince Hal-haters. Many of Shakespeare's characters seem aware of the range of potential selves buried within them, and readily slip into other roles. Especially for Shakespeare's women, dressing up as a man opens up opportunities to test forms of selfhood they might otherwise never have known. Rosalind in *As You Like It* can turn into an androgynous, flirtatious figure and organize everyone else's love lives; Portia, in *The Merchant of Venice*, can demonstrate her clever legal mind while testing the mettle of her fiancé. Only Cleopatra, the embodiment of theatricality, has no use for masquerade to flaunt her infinite variety: she is always in character. Personalities like these are acutely aware of their multiplicity: 'I am not what I am' is a line Shakespeare uses twice, in *Twelfth Night* (3.1.142) and in *Othello* (1.1.64), and one which is echoed by Hal, who reproaches that perennial player, Falstaff, with the words, 'thou art not what thou seem'st' (*King Henry IV*, Part 1, 5.4.135). All speakers in Shakespeare are only ever actors.

One way Shakespeare creates characters, and makes them convincing as unique individuals, is by giving them a distinctive voice. They are defined mainly by the way they speak. Even minor characters are characterized through their quirks of speech: Pistol's bombast and Nym's 'humours' in the second Henriad, Dogberry's malapropisms. Some characters use language in a way that goes against the grain of all assumptions. The savage Caliban, who Prospero claims is immune to the civilizing force of education, is given some of the most poetic lines of the play:

> Be not afeard. The isle is full of noises,
> Sounds and sweet airs that give delight and hurt not.
> Sometimes a thousand twangling instruments
> Will hum about mine ears; and sometimes voices,
> That if I then had waked after long sleep,
> Will make me sleep again; and then in dreaming,
> The clouds, methought, would open and show riches
> Ready to drop upon me, that when I waked
> I cried to dream again.
>
> (*The Tempest*, 3.2.136–44)

Othello, described in the opening scene in animal imagery as a copulating 'black ram' (1.1.87) and a 'Barbary horse' (110), confounds audience expectations when he expresses himself in gracious and elegant poetry. Throughout the play, the grandiose sweep of the Moor's rhetoric is juxtaposed with the coarse, pornographic language Iago indulges in – until Othello's language falls to pieces, together with his identity. To a greater extent than his contemporaries, Shakespeare honed the craft of presenting characters in the act of exploring their own thoughts. The soliloquies they deliver allow us to watch their minds at work. In fact, we observe them shaping their thoughts through their words, talking themselves into a certain frame of thought, or mood, to enable them to take action, devising roles for themselves, evolving and shifting their personalities from scene to scene. We watch them watching others and watching themselves. In Shakespeare, inward lives are closely bound up with language: people create themselves through the words they use. In one of the most incisive studies of how we became what we are, *Sources of the Self: The Making of the Modern Identity* (1989), the philosopher Charles Taylor has identified a number of features of the modern individual. These include a distinctive inner self, and a feeling of autonomy, which implies the freedom to choose one's own course of action, as well as a sense of disengagement from our natural surroundings. Characters in Shakespeare's plays are in this sense like us. They think they are in control of their own destiny, as we do; they are responsible for their own deeds, rather than steered by gods or spirits. They are doomed to fail because they are determined to follow their own, self-determined course – as Hegel puts it, they are 'free artists of themselves'. Or so they believe. They are perennially changing, however much they might claim to be the quintessence of constancy. They live in an increasingly disillusioned age in which God seems to have moved away and all there is is the world we live in, and other people. And they have an ironic, detached view both of themselves and of their environment, aware that whatever they do, one part of them is always in the wings, watching.

In his book *Contingency, Irony, and Solidarity* (1989), the philosopher Richard Rorty sees irony as the inescapable condition of modern humankind. Thinkers such as Nietzsche, Freud and Wittgenstein have demolished our cherished belief in a single, core identity. They have demystified our notions of language. As they have shown, language is not merely a tool we use to express ourselves and describe reality. Instead, it is a system that filters our access to reality and shapes our identity. But an ironic awareness of the fact that we are puppets of circumstance and chance, that our selfhood is a product of forces outside our control, does not mean that we cannot make commitments. For Nietzsche, the only purpose for humans in a world without universal truths was to cultivate their personalities – to live life as a work of art. Rorty, on the other hand, believes we can combine an ironic viewpoint on a personal level with a commitment to social justice in the public sphere. What we need to throw overboard is our hunger for one single, all-encompassing truth. And it is literature, he claims, that will help us to do so.

For Rorty, literature has a vital role to play in a disenchanted world. It fosters an awareness of the diversity of life, of the variegated points of view in humankind. Most of us experience only a narrow slice of life. It is through fictions, claims Rorty, that we learn about the attitudes of other people. We become conscious of the fact that there never is only one single story. Our own values are thrown open to scrutiny. And, by gaining an insight into the minds of others, we learn to understand ourselves. We begin to see the blindness of fictive characters and their casual cruelty to other people reflected in our own actions. In the final analysis, this leads to a politics of solidarity towards other human beings. A key advocate for the power of literature is Vladimir Nabokov, who in his Afterword to *Lolita* sets up the claim that art evokes 'curiosity, tenderness, kindness, and ecstasy'. As Rorty points out, the pleasure that literature provides is inextricably bound up with entering the lives of the myriad characters who people books or plays – which enables us to understand their pain and nurtures a sense of obligation towards others.

Or does it? What effect does the theatre really have on its audiences? A typical feature of Shakespeare's work is its sustained inquiry into the medium with which he worked. Exploring questions of theatricality was a staple of early modern drama, which abounded in asides to the audience, plays-within-plays, cross-dressing – boys playing girls playing boys – and in-jokes about the theatre. In more serious plays like *Hamlet*, the issue is endlessly dissected. Hamlet devises a play-within-the-play to entrap his uncle, but instead it casts doubt on all assumptions about the theatre. It is by no means clear that Claudius reacts to the play for the reasons Hamlet attributes to him, namely guilt at his crime. Perhaps what Claudius sees is a play in which a nephew, Lucianus, murders his uncle. He might well have felt vindicated in his suspicions about his own nephew as a dangerous terrorist. What does art do? Does theatre make anything at all happen? Once again, Shakespeare's plays offer no conclusive answer.

To be sure, sometimes illusions in the plays do serve a redemptive purpose: Prospero's playlets lead to reconciliation and renewal, at least for some; the plays directed by Don Pedro in *Much Ado About Nothing* deceive Benedick and Beatrice into falling in love with each other, a match that seems perfect to the spectators. In *The Winter's Tale*, Paulina stages the statue scene to reverse the Pygmalion myth and teach Leontes to recognize his wife as a woman of flesh and blood. And sometimes characters use fictions to serve their own purposes: in the same play Perdita cites the story of Proserpina only to make it clear that, unlike the mythic queen of the underworld, she intends to retain control of her own desire.

On the other hand, the characters watching plays onstage frequently miss the point – as is the case with the lovers in *A Midsummer Night's Dream*. They remain blind to the glaring parallels between the play-within-the-play and their own idiocy, and are blithely unaware of the perhaps tragic brink on which they are teetering. The smug courtiers in *Love's Labour's Lost* are no better, happy to jeer at the absurdity of less-noble characters immediately after having revealed their own folly. Hamlet, hungry for confirmation through art, learns nothing he didn't know already. He is no more capable of decisive action after 'The Mousetrap' than he was before.

The Romantics are right to point out that Shakespeare's art is imbued with irony. Shakespeare's plays offer a profusion of divergent outlooks that are often diametrically opposed to each other and call one another into question. Sometimes these conflicting viewpoints are articulated by wise fools; more often, they emerge through the way he crafts his plots or manipulates their endings. The plays are brimming with fascinating, exasperating characters, all of whom have their own take on reality, and speak in an endless variety of styles. They depict individuals busily looking into their own hearts and minds, but what they find is not necessarily what we see. We observe characters whose personalities are ambivalent and forever evolving, despite their firm belief in their stable identities. They are obsessed with spying and eavesdropping on each other, but, once again, what they discover is not what we perceive. They are often so self-deluded that they miss what is in plain sight. Sometimes, as in the case of the speaker or speakers in the *Sonnets*, they simply don't want to know. In Sonnet 138, the speaker responds to declarations of love by his beloved by remarking laconically, 'I do believe her, though I know she lies'; more painfully, we watch the speaker in Sonnet 42 go to tortuous lengths to explain that betrayal is no such thing, but a huge enrichment. And yet, one part of him is fully aware of the fact that the greater liar is himself – in Sonnet 152, the harsh pun on his 'perjured eye' brutally sums up his self-betrayal.

The undercurrent of irony that runs through Shakespeare's work spills over into a sceptical view of his own art. By continually drawing attention to the fact that they are fictions, and asking questions about the effects they might achieve, the plays open up avenues of inquiry that they refuse to resolve. Sometimes they seem to support Rorty's view that the only source of redemption is the human imagination. Sometimes, however, they show us how different people read the same story in radically different ways. For centuries, Shakespeare has been interpreted and cited in support of a bewildering array of worldviews ranging from the subversive to the reactionary. Artists and thinkers have been reading Shakespeare and re-creating him in a dazzling variety of shapes and forms. His work has become part of our common stock of cultural knowledge. Perhaps Shakespeare's art does offer the potential to help us achieve a sense of solidarity with other human beings. This might be a fellowship in sharing the same cultural memories. The novelist Joseph Conrad believed that art would outlive successive ideologies and political systems. In his 'Preface' to *The Nigger of the 'Narcissus'* (1897) he writes that the artist 'speaks to our capacity for delight and wonder, to the sense of mystery surrounding our lives; to our sense of pity, and beauty, and pain; to the latent feeling of fellowship with all creation – and to the subtle but invincible conviction of solidarity that knits together the loneliness of innumerable hearts: to the solidarity in dreams, in joy, in sorrow, in aspirations, in illusions, in hope, in fear'. Not only do audiences all over the world marvel, laugh, and cry at the same plays – Shakespeare's work offers a ground for a possible sense of communality based on shared dreams and aspirations.

What is undisputed is that Shakespeare has left us a treasury of stories and an astonishing range of storytelling techniques. As artists who mine him for inspiration know only too well, works of art are always bound up in a tissue of relations with other works. But artists are not the only people who create stories. Each of us weaves narratives for ourselves, making ourselves up as we go along – and we are hungry for fictions to quarry for our own purposes. For we always define ourselves in relation to others, be they real people or fictive characters. We plunder cultural scripts and literary paradigms to recreate ourselves, and shape our lives into narratives. We see the world through fictions, and grasp our lives as an evolving story.

Above all, Shakespeare's wealth of stories, characters, moods and language has the power to evoke an intense delight in the wonder and richness of life. The comedies articulate our fantasies of a golden world of love and happiness, however precarious; the tragedies offer visions of towering passions and the ironies of fate; the poetry evokes the poignancy and pathos of human relations. Shakespeare's legacy is a celebration of life in its endless variety. In his poem 'Snow' Louis MacNeice puts it in a nutshell:

> World is crazier and more of it than we think,
> Incorrigibly plural. I peel and portion
> A tangerine and spit the pips and feel
> The drunkenness of things being various.

William Shakespeare
1616–2016

Paul Edmondson

Imagine that you see him looking out
above you from a window at New Place,
there's music in his mind, the people shout
and cheer to see their hearts beat in his face.
His book, brimful with lovers, clowns and kings,
spills over, dances down his window sill –
a silken thread of ink still spinning sings
and weaves our tongues together with his quill.
Tonight his words will nest in rhyming trees,
quick syllables strike moonbeams on the land;
his pages, stirred with rhythms of the seas,
break tempests of the mind upon the sand:
    our muse of fire, water, earth and air
    in Stratford-upon-Avon – everywhere.